The Hidden Power of
SPEAKING *in*
TONGUES

MAHESH CHAVDA

Destiny Image® Publishers, Inc.
P.O. Box 310
Shippensburg, PA 17257-0310

"Speaking to the Purposes of God for This Generation
and for the Generations to Come"

ISBN 0-7684-2171-3

For Worldwide Distribution
Printed in the U.S.A.

12 13 14 15 16 17 / 16 15 14 13 12 11 10

This book and all other Destiny Image, Revival Press, MercyPlace, Fresh Bread, Destiny Image Fiction, and Treasure House books are available at Christian bookstores and distributors worldwide.

For a U.S. bookstore nearest you, call **1-800-722-6774**.
For more information on foreign distributors, call **717-532-3040**.
Or reach us on the Internet:
www.destinyimage.com

ISBN 978-0-7684-1357-1

CONTENTS

ACKNOWLEDGMENTS

Thanks . . .

- To my wife, Bonnie—helpmate, friend, and most committed intercessor on our pilgrimage in healing.

- To Karen Johnston, my secretary, who has given countless hours of diligent labor to this ministry and contributed much to the completion of the book— bless you for your devotion.

- To Rebecca Neilson, Jenna Orvin, and Kimberly Shead who worked tirelessly helping me complete this work.

Introduction

This book contains an amazing key that will help you unlock treasures of healing, victory, and restoration that you may have thought were out of reach for you. How well I remember the terrible cloud of darkness and depression that settled upon me many years ago. Thoughts of suicide welled up like a strong tidal wave. Into this deep darkness a supernatural light suddenly broke through and lifted me into a realm of amazing grace and triumph. A new song came into my life, and its melody and many variations of that melody have touched hundreds of thousands of people across the globe.

I know beyond a shadow of a doubt that if you have experienced dark clouds of defeat and depression, the truths in this book will help release a song of joy and the voice of triumph in your life. What song are you singing today? Is your step burdened? If you connect with the truths in this volume, you will begin singing a new song and know the Lord's promise, "to give [you] beauty for ashes, the oil of joy for mourning, the garment of praise for the spirit of heaviness" (Is. 61:3b).

There is a gift waiting for you that you simply need to unwrap. God's amazing love has arranged for you to have this gift. It is reserved just for you. This book is an invitation to you to receive your gift. It will never leave you. What it will do is take you from one realm of joy to another. I know it. I have experienced this personally. So can you.

Chapter One

THE LANGUAGE OF GLORY

I believe in the power of speaking in tongues. I believe because I have witnessed its power in my own experience as well as in the experiences of others. One night very late I began praying in tongues and prayed aggressively for nearly three hours. Although I did not know what I was praying for, I sensed that I was praying through to victory for something very important. I wasn't afraid or particularly in distress, just very intent to faithfully pray with the Lord until He released me.

When the burden lifted I got up and left my office to go to bed. Going down the hall I noticed the light was still on in my daughter Anna's room, where she was studying for college semester finals. I stuck my head in to say good night and felt impressed to ask Anna not to drive my car to school that day. "Take your mother's Jeep," I insisted. Anna normally drove my car to class in the mornings. I knew of no reason for my request other than the deep and distinct impression I felt. I learned long ago to pay attention to these promptings of the Holy Spirit. After I repeated my request a couple of times, Anna finally rolled her eyes at me and said, "Okay, Dad, I promise!"

A few hours later Anna was on her way to her class. That particular morning she decided to take a route she was not accustomed to. An early rain had left the road surfaces slippery. Blinded by the morning sun in her eyes, Anna lost control of the vehicle as she unexpectedly came upon a hairpin curve. The Jeep skidded off the road and slammed head-on into a tree at approximately 35 mph, pinning Anna inside. The vehicle was totaled.

By the time Bonnie and I were notified and arrived on the scene, an emergency rescue team was extracting Anna from the Jeep on a stretcher. Fire, police, and emergency rescue personnel were everywhere. One of them told Bonnie, "I've worked nearly 30 calls like this, and this is the first time the driver survived." We heard similar stories from other rescue personnel who were present. In their experience, accidents of this type almost always resulted in massive injuries or death. What we heard over and over that morning from officials on the scene were the words, "It's a miracle your daughter is alive."

After the ambulance left for the hospital, one of the police officers present pointed again at the demolished Jeep. "Those airbags saved her life," he said. Bonnie and I knew also that God and His angels had been on assignment. My car—the one Anna normally drove to class—was not equipped with airbags. Had she been driving my car that morning, the outcome might have been altogether different. As it was, Anna suffered bad breaks in both legs, but fully recovered with no permanent ill effects from her injuries.

That morning I understood why I had been so burdened in prayer just hours before. The Holy Spirit knew of the danger ahead of time and prompted me to pray in tongues until the burden lifted. One alert watchman can save an entire house. The thief who comes to steal, kill, and destroy will pass by a house where the watch lamps are brightly burning.

During nearly 30 years of ministry I have personally witnessed multiplied thousands of instances where people who have turned to Jesus Christ in repentance and faith after hearing the gospel preached have manifested confirming signs and wonders in their lives as evidence of the Lord's presence. Blind people have received their sight and deaf people their hearing. Lame people have walked and demonized people have been delivered. Many new believers, even those who have never heard of the Holy Spirit, have spontaneously received the baptism of the Spirit, evidenced by speaking in tongues. I particularly remember one overseas crusade in which thousands responded to the gospel. As I prayed over these new converts and welcomed the Holy Spirit, He swept over the crowd in a wave, and 50,000 began speaking in tongues at one time.

Over the last century the Church has seen an outpouring of the gifts of the Holy Spirit and of the presence and power of the Lord that are unparalleled since Pentecost. God is up to something big, and speaking in tongues is just one part—one indicator of what He is doing.

From the River to the Glory

For the better part of a decade now thousands of believers have been basking in the warm flow of a spiritual renewal that has become popularly known as "the river." Epitomized by the outpourings at the Toronto Airport Christian Fellowship in Toronto, Ontario, and the Brownsville Assembly of God in Pensacola, Florida, this latter-day visitation of the Spirit of God has resulted in many lost people being saved—their lives totally transformed by the power of God—and many more believers who have received a fresh touch from the Spirit—a deepening sense of His intimate presence.

As wonderful and refreshing as it is, "the river" is only the beginning. Signs are all around that God has opened a new phase, which we could call "the glory." Building on "the river" experience, "the glory" seeks to take us beyond it to even deeper levels of intimacy with the Lord and greater manifestations of His presence. It seeks to reconnect us to the kind of outpouring of the Holy Spirit that came at Pentecost, marking and empowering the Church to carry out Christ's commission to carry the gospel to every nation.

As believers in the twenty-first century, we are part of the last-days Church. It is highly possible that our generation or that of our children will witness the return of Christ. Jesus said, "And this gospel of the kingdom will be preached in all the world as a witness to all the nations, and then the end will come" (Mt. 24:14). There is no logistical or technological reason why that commission cannot be fulfilled within our lifetime. We have even now the means to carry it out. Jesus charged the Church with the mission of preaching the gospel and making disciples in every nation. That is her purpose, her very reason for existing as a body. Every endowment from God, every spiritual gift, every empowerment we receive from the Lord is to equip her for that mission.

The Church is the Bride of Christ, and part of the ministry of the Holy Spirit is to prepare the Bride for the coming of her Bridegroom. When Jesus comes to claim His Bride, she will appear before Him arrayed in the glorious garments of grace, faith, obedience, and holiness. By herself, the Bride can do nothing. It is the Spirit of God who anoints the Bride of Christ. As the day of the Bridegroom's return approaches, the Spirit's activity of preparation will increase. This is an awesome mystery. God is doing a mighty work in His people. He is transforming us into a Bride fit for His Son, and His agent in this transformation is the Holy Spirit.

As the preparer of the Bride, the Holy Spirit is like Abraham's servant in the Book of Genesis, who was the steward and administrator of everything that Abraham owned, and who Abraham sent to find and prepare a bride for his son Isaac. He went out and chose Rebekah, who became Isaac's wife. The Holy Spirit is like the king's eunuch in the Book of Esther who trained and taught Esther and prepared her to go before the king.

This is the same Holy Spirit who came on the Day of Pentecost, 50 days after the resurrection of Jesus and ten days after His ascension, and filled the 120 believers who were gathered together in that upper room in Jerusalem. He is the third Person of the Godhead, coequal with God the Father and Jesus Christ the Son. When the Spirit filled those believers at Pentecost, they began to speak in tongues. The Spirit's presence connected them with the heart and mind of God in a whole new way, and speaking in tongues was the "supernaturally natural" expression of that connection.

Speaking in tongues is "spirit talk," a language that connects us to the glory of God just as it did for those believers at Pentecost. As we move from "the river" into "the glory," tongues will continue to be a major part of the process.

Spiritual "Windtalkers"

Speaking in tongues is the language of glory, an outward manifestation of the fulfillment of Jesus' promise that the Holy Spirit would come to dwell permanently in the hearts and lives of believers. The Holy Spirit gave birth to the Church and part of that birth was tongues. The Church was born speaking in tongues.

When the Day of Pentecost had fully come, they were all with one accord in one place. And suddenly there came a sound from heaven, as of a rushing mighty wind, and it filled the whole house where they were sitting. Then there appeared to them divided tongues, as of fire, and one sat upon each of them. And they were all filled with the Holy Spirit and began to speak with other tongues, as the Spirit gave them utterance (Acts 2:1-4).

Not long ago, two events occurred in our country that brought greater public attention to one of the lesser-known stories of World War II. President George W. Bush awarded the Congressional Gold Medal, the highest civilian award Congress can bestow, to four surviving members of the original 29 "windtalkers"—Native Americans of the Navajo nation who served as Marines in the Pacific theater and who used their Navajo language as a communications code that the Japanese found impossible to break. At about the same time, a Hollywood motion picture named "Windtalkers" was released, which gave a fact-based but somewhat fictionalized account of the same story.

The word *windtalkers* refers to the Navajo way of speaking, a "talking into the wind." A Navajo code talker was assigned to each Marine division to provide secure communication between them free from interception by the Japanese. In what undoubtedly sounded like mere gibberish to the eavesdropping enemy, these "windtalkers" used their unique language to coordinate battle plans and strategy, call in artillery fire, and give status reports. They are credited with making significant contributions to the American victories on Guadalcanal, Iwo Jima, and other major battles on the islands of the Pacific.

This story of the Navajo windtalkers brought to my mind a connection with those believers long ago who talked into the "wind" of Pentecost. The Greek word *pneuma*, which is often translated "spirit," also means "breath" or "wind." The 120 believers gathered in that upper room heard "a sound from heaven, as of a rushing mighty wind," and they "began to speak with other tongues." These newly Spirit-filled believers were spiritual "windtalkers." They spoke in a new language that was like a "breath" of Heaven.

Just as the Japanese could not penetrate the code of the Navajo windtalkers, so the devil cannot break through the language of the Spirit. Speaking in tongues is a heavenly communication, a language that links us with the glory of God. It puts us in tune with His heart and mind. Just as the Navajo windtalkers alone could understand each other in their unique tongue, so also do spiritual windtalkers have a secure communication with the Lord, a special language or "code" that cannot be intercepted, understood, or subverted by the enemy. Speaking in tongues is the language of the realm of Heaven. The problem is that we have spiritualized and religionized it to such a point of controversy that it is easy to lose sight of its true nature and purpose—to connect us with the glory of the Lord.

Spiritual Power Is for Bearing Witness to Jesus

The last thing the risen Jesus said to His followers before He ascended to Heaven was:

But you shall receive power when the Holy Spirit has come upon you; and you shall be witnesses to Me in Jerusalem, and in all Judea and Samaria, and to the end of the earth (Acts 1:8).

Jesus' words contain two imperatives for His disciples: "You shall receive power," and "you shall be witnesses to Me." These two "you shalls" go together; either one is meaningless without the other. A witness to Jesus that has no spiritual power accomplishes nothing, and spiritual power that does not witness to Jesus has no purpose.

Every spiritual gift and other endowment of the Spirit, including speaking in tongues, is bestowed on believers for the ultimate purpose of equipping and enabling us to bear witness, both individually and corporately, to the saving work of Jesus Christ through His death on the cross and His bodily resurrection. Whenever we begin to focus on spiritual gifts for their own sake, whether tongues or anything else, we are headed for trouble. As Christians we are always in danger of slipping into one or the other of two extremes, both equally dangerous. Placing too little emphasis on the gifts and presence of the Holy Spirit robs us of power, while placing too much robs us of vision and direction because it takes our eyes off Jesus.

Before He went back to Heaven, Jesus charged His followers with a clear and specific commission:

Go therefore and make disciples of all the nations, baptizing them in the name of the Father and of the Son and of the Holy Spirit, teaching them to observe all things that I have commanded you; and lo, I am with you always, even to the end of the age (Matthew 28:19-20).

Our marching orders are to make disciples in every nation and teach them to obey Jesus. To enable us to carry out His command, Jesus promised to be present with us always, and His presence always brings His power. Jesus' presence with us enables us to proclaim the gospel with power and see lives transformed by His Spirit.

Mark records the same commission in slightly different form, but the implications are the same:

And He said to them, "Go into all the world and preach the gospel to every creature. He who believes and is baptized will be saved; but he who does not believe will be condemned. And these signs will follow those who believe: In My name they will cast out demons; they will speak with new tongues; they will take up serpents; and if they drink anything deadly, it will by no means hurt them; they will lay hands on the sick, and they will recover" (Mark 16:15-18).

Both forms of Jesus' commission stress the preeminence of bearing witness—of preaching the gospel and making disciples—and both promise the presence of the living Lord with His people. While Matthew focuses on the *fact* of Jesus' presence—"I will be with you always"—Mark *emphasizes* the evidence of His presence—"And these signs will follow those who believe..."

Luke likewise closes his Gospel with commissioning words from Jesus, and like Matthew and Mark, they focus on proclaiming the gospel throughout the world and on the empowering presence of the Lord that makes it possible:

Then He said to them, "Thus it is written, and thus it was necessary for the Christ to suffer and to rise from the dead the third day, and that repentance and remission of sins should be preached in His name to all nations, beginning at Jerusalem. And you are witnesses of these things. Behold, I send the Promise of My Father upon you; but tarry in the city of Jerusalem until you are endued with power from on high (Luke 24:46-49).

Our commission as believers is to preach to all nations "repentance and remission of sins" in Jesus' name. The "Promise of My Father" refers to the Holy Spirit, who descended upon and filled the believers on the Day of Pentecost, at which time they were "endued with power from on high." As Acts 2:4 makes clear, the *initial* evidence of the presence of the Holy Spirit in power was that the believers "began to speak with other tongues, as the Spirit gave them utterance." This set the stage for the preaching of the gospel to the thousands of pilgrims who were in Jerusalem for the festival.

In every instance, the release of spiritual power is inextricably bound up with the mission of bearing witness to Jesus. At the same time, speaking in tongues is clearly linked to the release of spiritual power as the initial outward manifestation of that power. Even then, however, its function was to enable the multinational crowd in Jerusalem to hear and understand the gospel, each in their own language, so that all who responded would be saved.

Here, then, is a solid and unchanging biblical principle: We are given spiritual power for the purpose of bearing witness to Jesus.

The Secret of Spiritual Power

In our generation more than ever before, the world is center stage to a spiritual battle of epic proportions between the powers of darkness and the powers of light. The Church is the vanguard for the powers of light on the earth, and we need weapons equal to the fight. Human wisdom and understanding are not enough. Jesus did not say, "You shall receive *knowledge* when the Holy Spirit has come upon you," nor did He say, "You shall receive *wisdom* when the Holy Spirit has come upon you." He said, "You shall receive *power* when the Holy

Spirit has come upon you." We do not need any more plans or schemes or formulas based on human wisdom or ingenuity; we are already stuffed to the gills with those. What we need is power—spiritual power.

Once, during a trip to Israel, I was praying with my family at the Garden Tomb when I felt the gentle nudge of the Spirit asking me rhetorically, "Where is the power of the Church? Where is the power in your life?"

There *is* a secret to the power. It is the secret that gives me the confidence of knowing every time I stand before 50,000 or 100,000 people or more during a crusade that God is going to heal several thousand of them. It is the secret that assures me that signs and wonders and miracles will flow. The Holy Spirit is the avenue, the agent through whom the power comes, but that power is released into and through our lives when certain conditions are met.

Paul of Tarsus knew the secret. He revealed it in his first letter to the church in Corinth:

> *And I, brethren, when I came to you, did not come with excellence of speech or of wisdom declaring to you the testimony of God. For I determined not to know anything among you except Jesus Christ and Him crucified. I was with you in weakness, in fear, and in much trembling. And my speech and my preaching were not with persuasive words of human wisdom, but in demonstration of the Spirit and of power, that your faith should not be in the wisdom of men but in the power of God* (1 Corinthians 2:1-5).

Did you catch that? The apostle Paul, one of the most highly educated and brilliant intellectuals of his day, determined to know nothing among the Corinthians except *Jesus*

Christ and Him crucified. That is the key. The secret to the "demonstration of the Spirit and of power" in Paul's preaching and ministry lay not in his great learning or in "persuasive words of human wisdom," but in the simple message of "Jesus Christ and Him crucified."

In our day we have so exalted excellence of human speech and profoundness of human wisdom that the basic truth of Jesus Christ and Him crucified often appears hopelessly rustic and archaic to our jaded and sophisticated minds, too simple a concept for a complex and enlightened age. It was just this kind of thinking that Paul had in mind when he wrote:

> *For the message of the cross is foolishness to those who are perishing, but to us who are being saved it is the power of God....For Jews request a sign, and Greeks seek after wisdom; but we preach Christ crucified, to the Jews a stumbling block and to the Greeks foolishness, but to those who are called, both Jews and Greeks, Christ the power of God and the wisdom of God* (1 Corinthians 1:18,22-24).

The secret to the release of spiritual power in our lives, our churches, and our ministries is to keep ourselves focused on the simple and basic message of "Jesus Christ and Him crucified." We have no other message for a lost and dying world. No other name under Heaven can bring salvation; only the name of Jesus. There is power in the name and the blood of Jesus. Sins are forgiven and lives are transformed in the name and by the blood of Jesus. Signs, wonders, and miracles flow when the gospel is preached and the name of Jesus is lifted up before the lost. Do you want to see the power of the Holy Spirit at work in you and through you? Then center your life on Jesus. Do not focus on the gifts but on the Giver; not on the power but on the One who is the source of the power.

We have two choices. Will our faith be in the wisdom of men or in the power of God? As long as we depend on human wisdom we will have a form of godliness but no power. If we emphasize peripherals—give primary attention to those things the Lord has said are secondary—we will also be disappointed in our desire to see God's Spirit move in power. We must keep the chief thing the chief thing: Proclaim Jesus Christ and Him crucified. That and nothing else is the secret to the release of spiritual power.

Connecting to God's Glory

God's desire for us is that we be a people in whom His glory can dwell, both individually and corporately. He wants to release us as carriers of His glory and His power. Through the Holy Spirit He has anointed us to carry the light of His truth and life, a light that none of the powers of darkness can withstand. As believers, each of us has been ordained of God to carry the mantle of His power and authority and be vessels through whom He can reveal His glory.

As part of that mantle, the Lord has imparted to us specific "grace gifts" to equip us for our role as agents of His power. One of the most personally useful of these is speaking in tongues. The gift of tongues is a marvelous endowment of the Holy Spirit. It helps us communicate directly with the Lord. Speaking in tongues is the main avenue to our flying higher and swimming deeper in the things of God. It is a special prayer language that connects us with the glory of God, enabling us to pray in the Spirit when we do not know what or how to pray in the weakness and limitation of our human minds. There is no limitation to praying in the Spirit because it taps into the limitless mind of God.

In our own human weakness, we often have difficulty expressing the true depth of our feelings and burdens to the Lord. Praying in the Spirit helps us overcome that difficulty. As Paul explained it to the Romans:

Likewise the Spirit also helps in our weaknesses. For we do not know what we should pray for as we ought, but the Spirit Himself makes intercession for us with groanings which cannot be uttered. Now He who searches the hearts knows what the mind of the Spirit is, because He makes intercession for the saints according to the will of God (Romans 8:26-27).

We may not know the will of God in every situation, but the Holy Spirit does, and intercedes for us accordingly. He aids us in prayer because He knows what is really going on in the realm that we do not see. He helps us aim our "prayer arrows" so that they always hit the target.

When the Spirit came the first time on the Day of Pentecost, He came with tongues. As He came then, He still comes today. Every true believer in Christ has the Holy Spirit living within, because the Spirit is the agent of God's saving grace and without His presence there is no salvation. Not every believer speaks in tongues, however. Some have been taught that the gift of tongues ceased around the end of the first century; others, that tongues are for some but not all. Speaking in tongues is certainly not *necessary* for salvation, but it *is* a wonderful asset for prayer and for helping us grow in effective ministry and in the grace and knowledge of the Lord. I believe, therefore, that it is available for every born-again follower of Christ who desires it and seeks it humbly and in faith.

When we pray in tongues the Holy Spirit gives utterance to things that we cannot express in human language. Because it is by nature an "unknown tongue," flowing in it calls for humility and submission on our part. We must be willing in faith to yield every part of ourselves to the King of glory—our body, mind, spirit, tongue, vocal cords. Everything yields to Jesus. To the natural mind this sounds foolish or even scary, but "the foolishness of God is wiser than men, and the weakness of God is stronger than men" (1 Cor. 1:25). That which we surrender to Jesus willingly, completely, and in humble faith He will bless and multiply exceedingly and abundantly beyond what we could ever do with our own resources.

Speaking in tongues carries many benefits for our spiritual lives. For one thing, it helps us grow more intimate with God. The more we speak in tongues the more we become possessed by the Holy Spirit. When we are exhausted and weary, speaking in tongues refreshes us in a marvelous way. It is like being in a flowing river on a hot day. Along with getting into God's Word regularly and spending quality time with Jesus on a daily basis, speaking in tongues is one of the best ways to get refilled.

Whenever we speak in tongues, we are magnifying and glorifying God because we are praying in the language of the Spirit—the language of glory. At the same time, we are also strengthening and building ourselves up in our faith: "But you, beloved, building yourselves up on your most holy faith, praying in the Holy Spirit, keep yourselves in the love of God, looking for the mercy of our Lord Jesus Christ unto eternal life" (Jude 1:20-21). Praying in the Spirit is a means by which we can build ourselves up, as well as our families, our homes, and our churches. Speaking in tongues is not just some kind of badge we pull out once in awhile as proof that we have been baptized in the Spirit. On the contrary, it is a wonderful tool and awesome spiritual weapon that God has given us, one that we do not utilize nearly often enough.

It is truly unfortunate that the practice of speaking in tongues has become such a point of contention in the Church. People on both sides of the issue have made the same mistake of focusing so much attention on the manifestation of tongues as to lose sight of the meaning behind it. As much a wonder as the gift of tongues is, it is merely an outward sign of an even greater wonder, that the living God has come down in the person of the Holy Spirit to literally and permanently dwell in the hearts of His people.

Pentecost was not an afterthought with God, but part of His plan from the beginning. Joel prophesied it centuries before the fact:

> *And it shall come to pass afterward that I will pour out My Spirit on all flesh; your sons and your daughters shall prophesy, your old men shall dream dreams, your young men shall see visions. And also on My menservants and on My maidservants I will pour out My Spirit in those days* (Joel 2:28-29).

The glory of the Lord came down on that first Pentecost after the death and resurrection of Jesus. In a similar manner, the glory of God descended on Mt. Sinai not long after He led the Israelites out of slavery in Egypt. We can better understand the significance of Pentecost if we understand the significance of what happened at Mt. Sinai. In many ways, Mt. Sinai foreshadowed Pentecost.

Chapter Two

MT. SINAI: FORESHADOWING PENTECOST

A couple of years ago I was leading a conference that was held under a large tent. This particular evening the tent was full with about 1,000 people present. At one point I began singing spontaneously under the leading of the Holy Spirit, using Paul's words from Second Corinthians:

> *Now the Lord is the Spirit; and where the Spirit of the Lord is, there is liberty. But we all, with unveiled face, beholding as in a mirror the glory of the Lord, are being transformed into the same image from glory to glory, just as by the Spirit of the Lord* (2 Corinthians 3:17-18).

As I started to sing people began to scream. Fortunately, they were not screaming about my singing! There was a big commotion in the middle of the crowd, and people were pointing to the top of the tent. There, just under the canvas, was a circling smoky cloud with shiny golden beams emanating from it, almost like gold lightning. The cloud stayed with us for about 30 minutes. We even recorded it on videotape, but the quality of our cameras was poor. It reappeared a few months later at another meeting, and this time we had better cameras.

All of the people who witnessed this cloud were awed by it and many were filled with the Holy Spirit afresh. We have made videotapes available for churches, and many pastors who have played the tape for their congregations report similar instances of recommitment among their people.

For me the appearance of this "glory cloud" is, in a small way, reminiscent of two related events recorded in Scripture: the descent of the Holy Spirit on the Day of Pentecost into the midst of the infant Church to infill and empower the believers, and the descent at Mount Sinai of the "glory cloud" of God's presence into the midst of the infant nation of Israel. Both involved the supernatural and direct presence of God with His people as well as divine-human interaction through speech. At Sinai God was establishing a nation; at Pentecost the Spirit of God was establishing a Church. Sinai was where God sought to connect directly with His people. Pentecost was the initial place where believers connected with the presence of God.

The first Christian Pentecost was not an isolated event but the culmination of a divinely preordained plan with its roots in early Jewish history. Many events in the Old Testament prefigure those of the New. A particular correlation exists between Mount Sinai and Pentecost. In many ways, Mount Sinai foreshadowed Pentecost.

Glory Like a Consuming Fire

From their earliest days as a nation, the Israelites learned to associate the glory and presence of God with cloud, smoke, and fire. As they moved from camp to camp in the wilderness, God led them with a pillar of cloud by day and a pillar of fire by night (see Ex. 13:21-22). When the Israelites camped at Sinai, God prepared to reveal His glory visibly to them so that they would obey Him and trust and follow Moses

as God's chosen leader. The people took two days to conse-
crate and prepare themselves, and on the third day the glory of
the Lord appeared on the mountain. Once again, He came with
cloud, smoke, and fire. It must have been an awesome sight.

> *Then it came to pass on the third day, in the morn-
> ing, that there were thunderings and lightnings, and
> a thick cloud on the mountain; and the sound of the
> trumpet was very loud, so that all the people who
> were in the camp trembled. And Moses brought the
> people out of the camp to meet with God, and they
> stood at the foot of the mountain. Now Mount Sinai
> was completely in smoke, because the Lord descend-
> ed upon it in fire. Its smoke ascended like the smoke
> of a furnace, and the whole mountain quaked great-
> ly. And when the blast of the trumpet sounded long
> and became louder and louder, Moses spoke, and
> God answered him by voice. Then the Lord came
> down upon Mount Sinai, on the top of the mountain.
> And the Lord called Moses to the top of the moun-
> tain, and Moses went up* (Exodus 19:16-20).

Following this scene are four chapters listing laws that
God gave to the Israelites through Moses, beginning with the
Ten Commandments in Exodus 20:1-17. The narrative contin-
ues in chapter 24 with Moses relating to the Israelites all the
words and judgments he had received from God. Afterwards,
the people offered up burnt offerings to the Lord and Moses
read the "Book of the Covenant" to the people, sprinkled
blood from the offerings on them, and consecrated them in the
covenant (see Ex. 24:3-8). When this was completed, God
summoned Moses to the top of the mountain in order to give
him the stone tablets of the law. Once again, the glory of the
Lord appeared in cloud and fire.

Now the glory of the Lord rested on Mount Sinai, and the cloud covered it six days. And on the seventh day He called to Moses out of the midst of the cloud. The sight of the glory of the Lord was like a consuming fire on the top of the mountain in the eyes of the children of Israel. So Moses went into the midst of the cloud and went up into the mountain. And Moses was on the mountain forty days and forty nights (Exodus 24:16-18).

Mount Sinai was the original "Pentecost," where God was setting apart for Himself a distinct and unique people, "a kingdom of priests and a holy nation" (Ex. 19:6a), who were to enjoy a unique relationship with Him and know His constant presence among them. On that day the glory of the Lord appeared to the children of Israel as a thick covering cloud and "like a consuming fire," and out of that cloud and fire the Lord spoke.

Centuries later, the glory of the Lord appeared like another kind of fire among another group of people. Instead of a mountain in the wilderness, the scene is an upper room in Jerusalem. Instead of former slaves newly liberated from Egypt, the people are willing bondservants of the King of kings, Jesus Christ, crucified, risen, and ascended, and are worshiping and waiting expectantly as He had commanded them to do.

When the Day of Pentecost had fully come, they were all with one accord in one place. And suddenly there came a sound from heaven, as of a rushing mighty wind, and it filled the whole house where they were sitting. Then there appeared to them divided tongues, as of fire, and one sat upon each of them. And they were all filled with the Holy Spirit

and began to speak with other tongues, as the Spir-
it gave them utterance (Acts 2:1-4).

The parallels are striking. On Mount Sinai the glory of
the Lord appeared "like a consuming fire"; at Pentecost it
appeared as "divided tongues, as of fire." At Sinai there were
"thunderings and lightnings"; at Pentecost, "a sound from
heaven, as of a rushing mighty wind." At Sinai God spoke to
the people through Moses; at Pentecost, the people spoke to
God "with other tongues, as the Spirit gave them utterance."
Both events centered on what I call the "thick presence" of the
Holy Spirit. In both cases the glory of the Lord came down,
and in the case of Pentecost, the believers were filled with the
Spirit and spoke in tongues. At Pentecost the filling of the
Spirit and speaking in tongues went hand in hand. This is why
I contend that tongues is the prayer language of the Spirit, a
heavenly language that connects us to the glory of God.

Pentecost: The Feast of Weeks

A vital connection between Mount Sinai and Pentecost has
been acknowledged since ancient times. According to a
rabbinical tradition that began with the great twelfth-century
Jewish rabbi and philosopher Maimonides, Pentecost is associated with the giving of the Law at Sinai and the birth of Jewish national existence. Jerome, a fourth-century "church
father," translator of the Vulgate, the Latin version of the
Scriptures, and one of the greatest scholars and intellectuals
produced by the early Church, also recognized the connection.
Comparing Pentecost with Mount Sinai, Jerome wrote, "There
is Sinai, here Sion; there the trembling mountain, here the
trembling house; there the flaming mountain, here the flaming
tongues; there the noisy thunderings, here the sounds of many
tongues; there the clangor of the ramshorn, here the notes of
the gospel-trumpet."

The oldest association of Pentecost with Mount Sinai derives from its identification with one of the three annual festivals of Israel. "Pentecost" is the Greek name for the Jewish "Feast of Weeks." Part of the Law given at Sinai stipulated three major agricultural festivals the Israelites were to celebrate every year: the Feast of Unleavened Bread, the Feast of Harvest (Pentecost) and the Feast of Ingathering (Tabernacles). Occurring 50 days after Passover, Pentecost celebrated the end of the grain harvest. Its primary focus was to express gratitude to God for a good harvest. Because it was a harvest festival, Pentecost was also known as the "feast of the firstfruits."

For Christians, the primary significance of Pentecost is the coming of the Holy Spirit to infill and indwell the Church. What connection is there between this event and the Feast of Weeks? Why did the Spirit come during a harvest celebration? When Peter spoke to the crowd in Jerusalem who had gathered because they had seen and heard the believers speaking in tongues, he explained that they were witnessing the fulfillment of a prophecy from the Book of Joel:

> *But this is what was spoken by the prophet Joel:*
> *"And it shall come to pass in the last days, says*
> *God, that I will pour out of My Spirit on all flesh;*
> *your sons and your daughters shall prophesy, your*
> *young men shall see visions, your old men shall*
> *dream dreams. And on My menservants and on My*
> *maidservants I will pour out My Spirit in those*
> *days; and they shall prophesy. I will show wonders*
> *in heaven above and signs in the earth beneath:*
> *blood and fire and vapor of smoke. The sun shall be*
> *turned into darkness, and the moon into blood,*
> *before the coming of the great and awesome day of*

the Lord. And it shall come to pass that whoever calls on the name of the Lord shall be saved" (Acts 2:16-21).

The prophecy of Joel that Peter quoted (Joel 2:28-32) was given originally in the context of a locust plague that had devastated Israel's crops, followed by a severe drought. Joel promised that God would bring agricultural restoration if the people gathered together in a sacred assembly and repented. On the heels of this promise, Joel then promised that God would pour out His Spirit on people without regard to age, gender, or social status, thus linking together the ideas of material and spiritual restoration.

With the killing of the paschal lamb, Passover commemorated Israel's deliverance from Egyptian slavery and at the same time marked the beginning of the harvest season with an offering of firstfruits. The Feast of Weeks, or Pentecost closed the season with a thanksgiving celebration for a fruitful harvest. Jesus Christ, the "Lamb of God who takes away the sin of the world" (Jn. 1:29b) was crucified during Passover. Three days later He was raised from the dead, becoming the "firstfruits of those who have fallen asleep" (1 Cor. 15:20b). Seven weeks later, during the end-of-harvest celebration at Pentecost, the Holy Spirit was poured out on the young Church, the gospel was proclaimed in power, and a great spiritual "harvest"—the first of the Church era—brought 3,000 souls into the Kingdom of God.

Pentecost is not just about manifestations. It is not just about a rushing mighty wind, or divided tongues of fire. It is not even just about speaking with other tongues as the Spirit gives utterance, as important as that is. Pentecost means many things. One major focus is the harvest, the empowering of the people of God to bring lost souls into His Kingdom. Another is the transformation of life through the power of the Holy Spirit. Pentecost is also about the anointing of a holy people set apart for God's service. In this sense, Pentecost focuses on the building of holy character.

God's Search for Character

When God called the nation of Israel out of Egyptian slavery into freedom, He had in mind the purpose of separating unto Himself a people whom He would love with a special love and who would return that love; people whom He could empower and into whom He could build divine character. He said to them:

> *You have seen what I did to the Egyptians, and how I bore you on eagles' wings and brought you to Myself. Now therefore, if you will indeed obey My voice and keep My covenant, then you shall be a special treasure to Me above all people; for all the earth is Mine. And you shall be to Me a kingdom of priests and a holy nation* (Exodus 19:4-6a).

God was grooming the Israelites to be children of royalty— His children—and He gave them laws and commandments to teach them how to live accordingly. Obedience to God's voice and faithfulness to His covenant were the signature evidences of the holy character that He was looking for.

Sadly, however, that character never really took root in the hearts of the Israelites. The history of that first post-Egypt generation of Israelites is a virtually unbroken litany of grumbling, discontent, and rebellion against God and against Moses, God's chosen leader. With a few exceptions, the Israelites never learned to think like royalty. In the midst of the freedom of God's guiding presence, they longed for Egypt where "we sat by the pots of meat and when we ate bread to the full..." (Ex. 16:3b), even though to return would mean slavery. Their obstinate refusal of God's command to cross into the land of Canaan and take it by force resulted in their being consigned to wander in the wilderness for 40 years until all of that rebellious generation had died (see Num. 14:1-38). The Israelites' lack of divine character prevented them from entering into intimate fellowship with the Lord and experiencing the joy of fulfilled purpose.

Pentecost signified the beginning of a whole new era, a new covenant of grace based on the blood of Jesus to supersede the old covenant of Law based on the blood of animal sacrifices. Through the birth, death, and resurrection of Christ, and the coming of the Holy Spirit, God intervened directly in the affairs of mankind in a totally unprecedented way. The holy character He sought would now be implanted in His people by transforming their hearts, something the Law of the old covenant was powerless to do:

> *I will give you a new heart and put a new spirit within you; I will take the heart of stone out of your flesh and give you a heart of flesh. I will put My Spirit within you and cause you to walk in My statutes, and you will keep My judgments and do them. Then you shall dwell in the land that I gave to your fathers; you shall be My people, and I will be your God* (Ezekiel 36:26-28).

The power to live as God requires comes from the indwelling presence of the Holy Spirit. It was for precisely this reason that the Spirit came at Pentecost:

> *For what the law could not do in that it was weak through the flesh, God did by sending His own Son in the likeness of sinful flesh, on account of sin: He condemned sin in the flesh, that the righteous*

requirement of the law might be fulfilled in us who do not walk according to the flesh but according to the Spirit (Romans 8:3-4).

All of us who are children of God through faith in Christ are being groomed to take our places as members of the royal family. The Holy Spirit is building in us the character of God and preparing us for our eternal destiny, which is to be the Bride of Christ. Unlike the ancient Israelites who never cast off their slave mentality, we must learn to comport ourselves like the princes and princesses we are. If we are to be the Bride of the King of kings, we must learn to think and act like royalty.

Thinking Like a Royal

I was born in Africa to Indian parents. My father died when I was five years old, so I never knew him very well. One of the things we discovered about my father after he died, however, was how truly generous a man he was. Long lists turned up of widows and orphans whom he had fed and cared for that no one ever knew about. Those fortunate souls never had to worry about their groceries; my father always took care of the bill. My father had a noble character and the bearing of royalty.

My mother was brought up in the royal houses of India. Before India became consolidated as one nation under British rule, it was made up of many small kingdoms. It was in that kind of environment that my mother grew up. Because of the royal influence around her, she developed a certain noble way of carrying herself and of thinking about herself and others. Much of her demeanor rubbed off on me.

Some of her clearest memories of those years were of playing around the king's throne while he was having an audience with some of the people in his kingdom. An audience with the king was a rare and precious thing, and those so fortunate would bow in honor as they entered his royal presence. The royal court was in session and these petitioners had been granted the opportunity to plead their case before the king. Perhaps a nearby landowner was illegally encroaching on their land and they were seeking relief, or perhaps they were simply seeking a favor. Whatever the situation, the king would listen.

It was customary when coming before the king to bring a gift. It didn't have to be anything great or magnificent, but was a gesture of respect and honor. After all, what could ordinary subjects give of value to a wealthy king who had everything? In return, the king always had a gift for his petitioner. Beside his throne was a large basket full of precious gems—emeralds, rubies, and diamonds. Some of the finest diamonds in the world come from India. The king would grab a handful of these gems, call the petitioner forward, and say, "Hold out your hand." Then he would place those gems in the hand of the astonished petitioner. What this meant to a humble peasant from a tiny village was that he and his family were taken care of for life. He no longer had to worry about anything, all because he had had an audience with the king.

This made a deep impression on my mother. All her life, whenever we had guests for dinner in our home, she never let them leave without giving them a little gift. As far as I can remember, the gift was always something made of gold—a gold necklace, gold earrings—something. Her years in the royal house had taught my mother to think like a princess, and it affected everything she did. Living in the environment of the king transformed her thinking.

As believers, our "royal house" is the Church of the Lord Jesus Christ. That is where the Holy Spirit disciples us in the glory, teaching us to think and behave like the royal children we are rather than poverty-stricken slaves. The Israelites who came out of Egypt never overcame their slave mentality and, as a consequence, forfeited their destiny. They had been under the yoke of slavery for so long that they found it impossible to think any other way.

Pentecost was where the believers first began to understand truly who they really were in Christ. Simon Peter, whose Spirit-inspired sermon that day brought 3,000 new people into the faith, described the Bride of Christ this way:

> *But you are a chosen generation, a royal priesthood, a holy nation, His own special people, that you may proclaim the praises of Him who called you out of darkness into His marvelous light; who once were not a people but are now the people of God, who had not obtained mercy but now have obtained mercy* (1 Peter 2:9-10).

We who know Christ are "a chosen generation, a royal priesthood, a holy nation"—God's special people. The Holy Spirit gives us ready access to the throne room of our King. For those fortunate individuals in my mother's memory, coming into the presence of the king was a once-in-a-lifetime opportunity. Through the Holy Spirit, we can have an audience with our King anytime, all the time, whenever we want. Speaking in tongues enhances our connection to the throne room. It is the language of the "royal house" of Heaven.

Tickled or Transformed?

At Sinai the "glory cloud" of God covered the mountain, and Exodus 24:18a says that "Moses went into the midst of the cloud and went up into the mountain." In First Corinthians 10:1-2 Paul says, "Moreover, brethren, I do not want you to be unaware that all our fathers were under the cloud, all passed through the sea, all were baptized into Moses in the cloud and in the sea." In these and similar passages the "cloud" represents the Holy Spirit. Entering into the midst of the cloud is like the baptism in the Holy Spirit that came at Pentecost.

All who know Jesus Christ as Savior and Lord have an open and continuing invitation from God to walk into the cloud of His glory. He wants us to experience Pentecost as a daily refreshing, not just know it as a singular event that occurred 2,000 years ago. His purpose is to build godly character in us: to transform us and make us into powerful, effective witnesses to His grace, mercy, and love. The choice we face is whether we want to be tickled or transformed.

Whenever there is a fresh move of the Holy Spirit bringing spiritual refreshing, renewal, or revival, there are always people who jump into the "river" and get caught up in the laughter, the "feel-good" sensations, the "warm fuzzies," or other manifestations for their own sake. These folks are more interested in being "tickled" by their Father than in being transformed by the Spirit.

Being tickled is fine up to a point, but the time comes when the Lord says, "Enough tickling. It's time to grow." Growth always involves transformation, and it always involves pain. That's why many believers would rather not bother. God did not save us to leave us the way we are. He did not give us the Holy Spirit just to tickle our fancy but to transform our heart. We are the Bride of Christ, and that means we are not to live for the world but for the Kingdom of our Bridegroom. Paul exhorted the Romans, "Do not be conformed to this world, but be transformed by the renewing of your mind, that you may prove what is that good and acceptable and perfect will of God" (Rom. 12:2). Instead of our being conformed to the world, God wants us "to be conformed to the image of His Son..." (Rom. 8:29b); instead of our having the mind of the world, He wants us to have the "mind of Christ" (1 Cor. 2:16b).

Character never forms in a vacuum. It grows out of the crucible of challenge, difficulty, hardship, struggle, and pain. God allows and uses these things to test the spirit and character of the Bride. Those who are interested only in tickling often will slip away when real challenge comes. Just as Moses walked into the cloud and came out with his face shining with the glory of the Lord, God challenges us to walk into the cloud and be similarly transformed.

This transformation is real and it is readily available, but it does not happen overnight. It takes time. God is committed to transforming us into the Bride of Christ, and He always completes what He begins. As Paul assured the Philippian Christians, "He who has begun a good work in you will complete it until the day of Jesus Christ" (Phil. 1:6b). The process will challenge everything in us. It will require patience, faithfulness, obedience, and the humble willingness to wait on the Lord.

The Character of Waiting

In the days between His resurrection and ascension, Jesus appeared numerous times to His followers, comforting them, encouraging them, and giving them instructions. Central to these instructions was the command to *wait* until the Holy Spirit was sent from the Father as He had promised:

> *"Behold, I send the Promise of My Father upon you; but tarry in the city of Jerusalem until you are endued with power from on high." And He led them out as far as Bethany, and He lifted up His hands and blessed them. Now it came to pass, while He*

blessed them, that He was parted from them and carried up into heaven. And they worshiped Him, and returned to Jerusalem with great joy, and were continually in the temple praising and blessing God (Luke 24:49-53).

And being assembled together with them, He commanded them not to depart from Jerusalem, but to wait for the Promise of the Father, "which," He said, "you have heard from Me; for John truly baptized with water, but you shall be baptized with the Holy Spirit not many days from now."... "But you shall receive power when the Holy Spirit has come upon you; and you shall be witnesses to Me in Jerusalem, and in all Judea and Samaria, and to the end of the earth." Now when He had spoken these things, while they watched, He was taken up, and a cloud received Him out of their sight....Then they returned to Jerusalem from the mount called Olivet, which is near Jerusalem, a Sabbath day's journey. And when they had entered, they went up into the upper room where they were staying: Peter, James, John, and Andrew; Philip and Thomas; Bartholomew and Matthew; James the son of Alphaeus and Simon the Zealot; and Judas the son of James. These all continued with one accord in prayer and supplication, with the women and Mary the mother of Jesus, and with His brothers (Acts 1:4-5,8-9,12-14).

In obedience to Jesus' command, His followers waited for the fulfillment of His promise. This waiting instilled eager, expectant anticipation in their spirits and built character in their hearts. It was an active waiting: They worshiped the Lord, praised and blessed God continually in the temple, and gathered in the upper room where they "continued with one accord in prayer and supplication."

Paul states in First Corinthians 15:6a that at one point the risen Jesus "was seen by over five hundred brethren at once," yet on the day of Pentecost, only 120 were present in the upper room. Where were the rest? Scripture does not say, but it is at least possible that many of the others were unwilling to wait, or were distracted from following the Lord, or simply drifted away. Some may have been more interested in being tickled than in being transformed. Whatever the reason, those who were absent missed out on the blessing. It is the ones who *waited* who received the promise.

The Church of Jesus Christ was birthed in the womb of the glory of God. As those patient, expectant believers met together in one accord in that upper room, a sound like a rushing mighty wind filled the house and divided tongues as of fire rested upon each of them. They were filled with the Holy Spirit and began to speak in tongues as the Spirit enabled them.

Waiting on the Lord strengthens faith and builds character. If we are willing to tarry, watch, and pray, we can enter into the midst of the "cloud" of God's glory. God likes that kind of "stubbornness," and He will pour out His Spirit.

We need to be hungry and thirsty for the Lord and be together in one accord, so the glory of God can come down. There's something powerful about being in one accord. When we are in one accord, the glory comes! We can expect a supernatural, heavenly fire to fall from Heaven that has the ability to burn away all our impurities of mind and spirit and transform us from the people we are into the people God wants us to be. Pentecostal fire can transform us into the Bride of Christ, beautifully adorned and without spot or blemish, ready to receive her Bridegroom. Just look at Simon Peter. He spent three and one-half years with Jesus, hearing Him teach and watching Him heal diseases and cast out demons, yet when the crunch came, he denied the Lord. Pentecost changed him in a matter of minutes. The power of God came upon Peter in that rushing mighty wind and those tongues of fire and transformed him forever. It can do the same for us.

The original "Pentecost" at Mount Sinai instituted the old covenant of Law sealed by the blood of animal sacrifices, which had no power to remove sin, but symbolized and foreshadowed the blood of Jesus, whose death on the cross would usher in a new covenant of grace. This new covenant is infinitely superior to the old. First of all, where the blood of animals could do nothing about sin, the blood of Jesus has the power to cover and wash away our sin, leaving us clean and whole before God. Secondly, under the old covenant God remained essentially apart from His people, His Spirit coming only upon certain persons at certain times for certain purposes. With the coming of the new covenant and the miracle of Pentecost, the living God now abides permanently in the hearts of His people through the indwelling of His Holy Spirit. This is unprecedented in all of human history.

The outpouring of the Holy Spirit at Pentecost was not an "addendum," not an amendment or afterthought to God's original plan, but of fundamental importance in and of itself. God's purpose in the new covenant was to redeem and establish a unique people who would be His own special possession. Their uniqueness would lie in the fact that they would be a people who were filled with the very breath of God Himself. They would be baptized with His Spirit.

Chapter Three

OPENING THE PROMISED GIFT

One of the joys of the holiday season for me is joining my family in making preparation for the festivities. I particularly enjoy watching gifts being wrapped. Have you ever had a Christmas present given to you where the wrapping was so beautiful that you didn't want to open it? The package is so stunning and wrapped with such great care that you just want to leave it as it is. Sometimes the outside is as impressive as the inside. No matter how attractive the exterior is, however, we have to open the gift to use it and make it ours.

Unfortunately, this is the same attitude many Christians have toward their faith. The greatest gift that we have been given, and which every believer in Jesus needs to open, is the precious gift of the Holy Spirit. It simply won't do to just stand back and say, "Hey, look at that wonderful gift. Isn't it lovely? I'm so thankful for it!" The Bible mentions many gifts, but for thousands of years the Father and the Son have been looking to bless humanity with this one thing. Jesus called it "the promise of the Father" (Lk. 24:49). The Father and Son have made this "promise" of the Holy Spirit available to all of us who are believers, but we must receive the gift. We must open it and make it our own.

God paid a very high price indeed to make this gift available: the very life of His Son. This beautifully wrapped gift is for each one of us. Everyone who believes can receive. God is no respecter of persons. In John 14:16-17, Jesus promised, "I will pray the Father, and He will give you another Helper, that He may abide with you forever—the Spirit of truth, whom the world cannot receive, because it neither sees Him nor knows Him; but you know Him, for He dwells with you and will be in you."

According to Acts 2:38 there are three steps for entering into the Kingdom of God. "Then Peter said to them, 'Repent, and let every one of you be baptized in the name of Jesus Christ for the remission of sins; and you shall receive the gift of the Holy Spirit.' " That sounds simple enough: repent, be baptized, and be filled with the Holy Spirit. These actions are a doorway to all the many gifts God has stored up for us.

The Fullness of the Spirit

When we first receive Jesus as our Savior, we also receive the Holy Spirit, who helps us become new creations in Christ. However, when we receive the *baptism* of the Holy Spirit, we receive the *fullness* of the Spirit. These two experiences, new birth and baptism in the Holy Spirit, should happen together, one after the other. Doctrinal problems have often prevented people from receiving the infilling of the Holy Spirit after their new birth experience. This, however, is not the New Testament pattern where believers received the infilling of the Holy Spirit as soon as they received Christ:

While Peter was still speaking these words, the Holy Spirit fell upon all those who heard the word. And those of the circumcision who believed were astonished, as many as came with Peter, because the gift of the Holy Spirit had been poured out on the Gentiles also. For they heard them speak with tongues and magnify God. Then Peter answered, "Can anyone forbid water, that these should not be baptized who have received the Holy Spirit just as we have?" (Acts 10:44-47)

A further example is found in Acts chapter 19:

And it happened, while Apollos was at Corinth, that Paul, having passed through the upper regions, came to Ephesus. And finding some disciples he said to them, "Did you receive the Holy Spirit when you believed?" So they said to him, "We have not so much as heard whether there is a Holy Spirit." And he said to them, "Into what then were you baptized?" So they said, "Into John's baptism." Then Paul said, "John indeed baptized with a baptism of repentance, saying to the people that they should believe on Him who would come after him, that is, on Christ Jesus." When they heard this, they were baptized in the name of the Lord Jesus. And when Paul had laid hands on them, the Holy Spirit came upon them, and they spoke with tongues and prophesied (Acts 19:1-6).

This is the way it happened for me. I had received Jesus, but had not heard much about the Holy Spirit. What I had heard was all very negative. People kept telling me, "He doesn't do this anymore." In the Book of Acts, however, we find that anytime anyone received the Holy Spirit, speaking in tongues followed. Furthermore, the Scripture indicates that those who received the Holy Spirit did so after first having heard the Word of God. Paul confirms this in Galatians 3:2 when he asks, "This only I want to learn from you: Did you receive the Spirit by the works of the law, or by the hearing of faith?"

When we are filled with the Spirit, the outward manifestation of this gift is speaking in tongues. The New Testament reveals this as the will of God for all believers. Paul told the Corinthians, "I wish you all spoke with tongues, but even more that you prophesied" (1 Cor. 14:5), and "If anyone thinks himself to be a prophet or spiritual, let him acknowledge that the things which I write to you are the commandments of the Lord" (1 Cor. 14:37). What Paul wrote is part of the canon of Scripture. It is the divine Word of God, His will for every believer's life.

The receiving or infilling of the Holy Spirit is a distinct second experience:

> *Now when the apostles who were at Jerusalem heard that Samaria had received the word of God, they sent Peter and John to them, who, when they had come down, prayed for them that they might receive the Holy Spirit. For as yet He had fallen upon none of them. They had only been baptized in the name of the Lord Jesus. Then they laid hands on them, and they received the Holy Spirit (Acts 8:14-17).*

Even though the filling of the Spirit is a separate experience from salvation, it can happen almost simultaneously with it. I have seen people immediately start speaking in tongues when they receive Jesus, sometimes without my even praying for it. Hundreds of times I have witnessed people praying, "Oh Jesus, I receive you," and then immediately start praising God in unknown tongues. Often I have said, "Lord, I haven't even prayed for them to receive the Holy Spirit!" That is completely beside the point. The Lord is under the impression that He is God, and if He is in a hurry to fill them, who am I to object?

I have seen total heathens receive Jesus: prostitutes and professors, prime ministers and plumbers, Hindus and Muslims, high and low, rich and poor all receive Jesus with the infilling of the Holy Spirit. I have seen hundreds of children receive the Spirit, and as the river starts bubbling out, tears start covering their cheeks, their faces suffused with indescribable joy and glory.

I have seen many hardened sinners come to Christ and watched as their visage literally changed when they received the infilling with speaking in tongues. One evening in a city on the eastern seaboard of the United States, twelve prostitutes gave their lives to Christ. The ravages of drug addiction were clearly visible, including the needle marks from heroin use. With no one behind them, or anyone touching them, they received the Holy Spirit and started speaking in tongues. Gently they all fell back on the floor, and to the amazement of all of us watching, all the needle marks on their arms disappeared instantly.

Many times, people who are filled with the Spirit have been thirsting for many years for a touch from the living God. Some of these people who were in their forties, sixties, and even seventies had never before had even one drink of the Holy Spirit. The infilling of the Holy Spirit is like taking your first drink of water after being thirsty for years. Jesus Himself compared receiving the Holy Spirit to a drink of water: " 'If anyone thirsts, let him come to Me and drink. He who believes in Me, as the Scripture has said, out of his heart will flow rivers of living water.'" But this He spoke concerning the Spirit" (Jn. 7:37b-39a). The person we come to is Jesus and the drink we take is the Holy Spirit. As we drink, the rivers of living water begin to bubble up. The only requirement for being filled with the Spirit is to be thirsty for more of God.

Believe and Receive

I received the Lord Jesus Christ as my Savior many years ago. He was gracious to me as a young aristocratic Hindu gentleman. At the age of 16 I experienced a mighty touch from the Lord wherein after reading the Bible my spirit was taken to Heaven. I describe this experience at length in my first book, *Only Love Can Make A Miracle*. In my vision I saw Heaven, walked the streets of gold, heard the most heavenly singing, and saw the most glorious array of rainbow-hued lights, and flowers with colors I didn't even know existed. There in that heavenly place I met the Lord Jesus Christ and because of that experience, the next day received Him as my Savior. Years passed but no one ever told me that I could receive the infilling of the Holy Spirit. I had received Jesus, but had not been filled with the Spirit. I believed in the Bible, I had been baptized, and I was aggressively serving the Lord. Slowly I began to move into intellectualism and gradually walked away from a committed life in Christ. I was still a Christian, but I was not enthusiastic about the Lord and had become very disappointed in the Church.

One day I received the news that my mother was dying of a terminal disease. I was a graduate student in Texas and my mother was in England. She was dying and I had no money to go see her. We had not parted on the best of terms, which made matters worse. She was a proud Hindu lady, raised up in the royal houses of India, and her son had left the Hindu faith to believe in the Lord Jesus Christ. She was not very pleased with what I had done. Now, years later, she was dying and asking to see me, but I could not afford to go. Any money I made went to pay for college and food. I was broken, defeated, and at the end of my resources. My heart deeply saddened, I wept uncontrollably for three days. I felt so ashamed.

On the third night, when I went to sleep I was suddenly back in that same heavenly place enveloped in the presence of the Lord. Surrounding the Lord was the Shekinah glory, like golden glory all around Him. Living beams of light emanated from Him. Songs of glory surrounded Him like anthems of worship and holiness. As Jesus came towards me, He put His hands on my shoulders, and I found myself singing anthems of praises to Him in a language I did not understand. For hours I was in that presence, singing.

When I woke up the next morning, my hands were folded tightly in an attitude of worship. It felt as though the atmosphere of glory still surrounded me, and I started worshiping the Lord Jesus again. As I did so, a gust of wind came into my room and blew the door open. I began taking deep breaths of this wind. Something was pouring into me like liquid love. I was bubbling over in my innermost being to the point that I had to open my mouth and let it out. It came out as a song in a language I did not understand.

At this time in my life I was very proud of being an intellectual, so I began to argue with myself saying, "This is crazy. What are you doing? You're speaking in a language that you don't understand!" Then I said back to myself, "It feels so great. I have never felt like this before in my life. I'm going to sing some more." I sang for about an hour and 20 minutes without a break. I was in the glory, saturated in a love that I had never felt before.

In those days the only other spiritual person whom I knew and respected was a Catholic nun who was taking graduate courses with me. I remember running up to her the next day and saying, "Sister Marsha. Am I going crazy?" As I described my experience to her she opened her eyes wide and started jumping up and down and saying, "Praise the Lord brother. You've been baptized in the Holy Ghost." She was a Spirit-filled nun!

Two days later, the word of the Lord came. As I was praying in tongues I had a strong impression that "Jesus Christ is the same yesterday, today, and forever." Again the word came on the song, "Jesus is the same yesterday, today, and forever. Jesus is the same yesterday, today, and forever." I started to sing that and then I said, "Lord, what do you mean?" The Holy Spirit answered, "It means, pray for your mother's healing. Jesus is the healer, the same yesterday, today, and forever." I started arguing the intellectual points again, "He doesn't do this anymore." I desperately needed that word. I could have approached it in an intellectual manner, or I could receive it like a desperately hungry person. I chose to receive it as a desperately hungry person.

I began praying earnestly for my mother, and a few days later I received the news that she had been healed completely of her bone cancer; from the top of her head to the tip of her toes. She lived for another 23 years, during which I had the chance to see her and lead her to Jesus Christ.

If you are trained in the kind of thinking that says, "The Lord doesn't do this anymore," I would say to you, "Stop arguing and receive." You will never be able to understand or fathom the mysteries of God. Jesus is a mystery. The cross is an awesome mystery. Just receive the gift of the Holy Spirit. Believe and receive your miracle.

This is not something we have to beg the Lord for. The Holy Spirit is a free gift through Jesus Christ. God has already made up His mind to pour out His Spirit and it is for us to receive. If we are children of God, we can simply ask and receive. Luke 11:10 says, "For everyone who asks receives, and he who seeks finds, and to him who knocks it will be opened." If we ask, we receive; if we seek, we will find; if we knock, it will be opened to us. When we ask for the Holy Spirit to come, we must welcome Him. I aggressively welcome His presence as often as I can into my life, into my home, into my ministry, for my children, for the Church, and for the nations. We can invite Him to do that because He is a gentleman, and as we invite Him, He will come in.

The coming of the Holy Spirit affects different people differently. Some receive very quietly. Some feel deep emotion. Some feel unspeakable joy, breaking forth in laughter, while others cry tears of thanksgiving. Some may feel drunk, behaving as the disciples did on the day of Pentecost. At the time of infilling, some get gloriously delivered from addictions to alcohol or tobacco. One thing is common to all who genuinely receive the Holy Spirit. As in my own experience, they all feel a deeper love for Jesus Christ than ever before. For me, the overwhelming sense of love was as much a supernatural manifestation of the Holy Spirit as was speaking in tongues. When I hear about people or cultures struggling with racism or anti-Semitism my comment often is that they need to be filled with the Holy Spirit. The true Spirit infilling results in hearts overflowing with love so that there is no place for hatred and bigotry.

When I was filled with the Spirit, I wanted to obey and please Jesus more than anything else. This should never make us feel prideful. God gives grace to the humble (see Jas. 4:6). My experience made me all the more humble and hungry for more of His wonderful presence. I was constantly singing, making up songs of praise on every occasion, anxious to serve in any capacity. My initial experience of infilling led me to ask if I could serve those in need around me in any manner possible, even if it was simply babysitting, cleaning homes, or even cleaning bathrooms! Soon after my infilling, the Lord sent me to be a servant of the most severely mentally handicapped youngsters at a state institution. That is when the miracles of healing began in earnest in my ministry.

The Chimpanzee School of Theology

Recently we suffered a bad ice storm in Charlotte. My home was without electricity or heat for several days. One evening as I was bundled up in my study, trying to work in the cold, my wife, Bonnie, came in. She looked at me curiously, noticing that I was chilled from head to toe. As she glanced from me to the "decorative" wood stove in the room, and then back to me, she said, "Mahesh, you know, with some logs and matches you could light that thing and be quite warm in here!"

Now, the way my mind works is that once I get an impression about something that's the way it stays for the next few years. It registers only one way and somehow it had registered in my brain that this wood stove did not work anymore and we were just using it ornamentally. I opened the door of the stove, filled it with wood, newspaper, and a starter log, and lit the mixture. I shut the door and lo and behold, it started firing up! It said, "Hello! I have been waiting for you. Why haven't you lit me up all this winter?" That stove heated up so well that even Bonnie came back in and warmed her hands. Soon it had warmed my entire study and was even beginning to warm the whole house.

If I had kept my initial impression about the wood stove, that it had worked at one time but was not working now, I would have remained cold. In the same way, Christians for centuries have been deprived of the warmth of the Spirit's work in their lives because of being taught that "Jesus stopped doing this a long time ago." As a result, many of us grow up in our spiritual walk ignorantly believing this to be the truth, all the while remaining cold and lifeless. Perhaps someone comes along and says, "Hey! It's working. You can be warm, you can be blessed." When this happens, we can receive the promise and renounce the lie.

Lewis Hastings, a British explorer of the late nineteenth century, noted in his explorations of Africa that his guide shared unusual insight into the behavior of chimpanzees. In the jungles of Angola there were often clearings where sticks had been carefully piled as if to make a good fire. When Hastings asked his guide how these things came to be there and why the sticks were so neatly arranged, he was astounded by the answer. Chimpanzees had gathered them! In Angolan, the word *chimpanzee* means "mock man." Hastings' guide told him that even though the Chimpanzees had piled the sticks and done it well, that was all they could do because they were missing the fire. Chimpanzees had seen men build a fire for cooking and for protection from wild animals. They were able to copy men's actions in building the fire heap and even gathered around waiting for something to happen. Their wait was in vain, however, because they did not have the fire itself. They would sit for hours but could not start a real fire; the needed spark was absent.

On the day of Pentecost, spiritual fire fell on the Church and the believers were filled with the Holy Spirit. This is Scripture; this is history. Yet, today there are "mock men" who don't know how to start the fire and who have never experienced the real fire, but try to tell us why we don't need the fire and why God doesn't give the fire anymore. This is what I call the "chimpanzee" school of theology.

The fire has been real in my life. Our first son, Ben, was given up for dead after his birth. There was little hope he could live due to a congenital birth defect in his urinary system. I saw him suffering in the most terrible way. After his last surgery he was screaming in terrible pain. After hours of Ben's suffering in agony, suddenly the nurses, Bonnie, and myself saw the glory of the Lord come. A glorious golden light surrounded Ben's crib as God literally recreated his nearly dead kidneys. Today he is a healthy, active 23-year-old in graduate school who loves the Lord and wants to serve Him. My wife and I have seen the real fire fall, where the presence of God has come and gloriously healed and delivered our children. I don't need someone to tell me God's supernatural fire does not fall any longer.

The fire of God is real and those who are hungry and thirsty will seek out that fire. Regrettably, there is a school of thought that causes people to be afraid of the Holy Spirit by instilling a mistrust of the heavenly Father. How unfortunate! Our Heavenly Father is the most trustworthy person in the universe. John 3:16 says, "For God so loved the world that He gave His only begotten Son." In Matthew 7:9-11 Jesus says, "Or what man is there among you who, if his son asks for bread, will give him a stone? Or if he asks for a fish, will he give him a serpent? If you then, being evil, know how to give good gifts to your children, how much more will your Father who is in heaven give good things to those who ask Him!"

If we ask for the Holy Spirit, the Lord surely will give us the Holy Spirit. The Holy Spirit is the third person of the Godhead. Just as the Father and the Son are all compassion, all love, all mercy, so also is the Holy Spirit. He is gentle, He is gracious, He is loving, He is merciful. He doesn't come to bully people and overwhelm them. I've often heard that people are advised to be careful of the Holy Spirit or else they may go crazy. These are libels and slanders by the spirit of antichrist against the Church receiving the infilling of the Holy Spirit and moving in His power.

In addition, some people have asked me, "Pastor, I've been told that tongues have ceased because 'the perfect' has come and I don't need to speak in tongues." I query back, "What is 'the perfect?' " They answer, "The Bible." Let us for a moment examine this misunderstanding. In First Corinthians 13:8-10, Paul writes, "Love never fails. But whether there are prophecies, they will fail; whether there are tongues, they will cease; whether there is knowledge, it will vanish away. For we know in part and we prophesy in part. But when that which is perfect has come, then that which is in part will be done away."

Paul was giving instruction in this chapter to stop some of the abuses of the gift of tongues that was occurring in the Corinthian church. His counsel was for them to focus on the eternal and not overemphasize the temporal. He encouraged them to pursue love as the paramount thing above all other gifts of the Spirit. At the return of the Lord, gifts would cease, whether prophecies, words of knowledge, or other gifts. Love would remain the constant.

Verse 12 says, "For now we see in a mirror, dimly, but then face to face. Now I know in part, but then I shall know just as I also am known." Therefore, the mirror is God's Word, the Bible. We dimly know the Lord through this mirror, but at His return, we will see Him face-to-face. It is illogical to say we will see the Bible face-to-face, but it is the Lord who we will see face-to-face in our glorified bodies. At that time, prophecies and other gifts will all be swept away in the presence of the King of Glory, the Lord Jesus. However, until that time, all gifts, including tongues, will be valuable tools for building up of the Kingdom of God.

A Gift for All Believers

I am not writing these things simply for the sake of argument. In my days of exalting the intellect, I debated with the best of them; Harvard, Cornell, and other Ivy League intellectuals. When I was filled with the Spirit, however, the Lord impressed upon me that soulish arguing and debating of doctrine is a work of the flesh. I have no interest in getting into controversies and arguments about speaking in tongues. If everything is wonderful in your life and you are happy and satisfied with all that you have in God, bless you. If, however, you are hungry for more of God, then I urge you to get more of the anointing and power of the Holy Spirit.

Speaking in tongues is the hidden key to moving in the power and anointing of the Holy Spirit. It is no wonder that the devil has fought against speaking in tongues. Those who are hungry and thirsty for the Lord can trust the promise of Jesus. It is real and it is for today because "Jesus Christ is the same yesterday, today, and forever" (Heb. 13:8). In our mass evangelism campaigns in Africa, I have had the privilege of seeing crowds of more than 50,000 at once receive the baptism of the Holy Spirit with speaking in tongues. It is quite something to behold.

Those who speak in tongues often will operate in other gifts as well. For example, they will lay hands on and pray for the sick according to Mark 16:15-18. Those who do not regularly speak in tongues also will not normally move in other gifts. In fact, they frequently will oppose participation in other gifts. Baptism in the Holy Spirit with speaking in tongues certainly seems to be the entrance to moving in other gifts. This is probably why the enemy of revival, satan, will fight so hard to discredit those who move in tongues and other gifts. If satan cannot discourage people from receiving the baptism of the Holy Spirit with tongues, he will try to bring discredit to the movement of the Spirit by pushing a few people into fanaticism, which often results in delusional action and an exaggerated sense of prophetic calling.

What is the criterion for receiving the Holy Spirit? Jesus said simply, "He who believes in Me…" (Jn. 7:38). Belief in Jesus as Savior and Lord is the criterion. Receiving the Holy Spirit is not a privilege reserved only for prophets, evangelists, pastors, or other leaders; every believer is eligible. The Holy Spirit is for "he who believes." No advanced degree is required. Male or female, rich or poor, young or old, it does not matter: anyone who believes can be filled with the Spirit. God is no respecter of persons (see Acts 10:34).

It is important for us to meditate on these things, chew on them, repeat them and proclaim them into the heavenlies. We need to absorb these truths into our very being, not only for us but also for our children and our children's children. Acts 2:39 says, "For the promise is to you and to your children, and to all who are afar off, as many as the Lord our God will call." The divine administrator of all the promises of God is the Holy Spirit. He holds the key to unlock the door. All the promises are yes and amen to us and to our families (see 2 Cor. 1:20).

The New Testament gives other evidence that the baptism of the Holy Spirit with speaking in tongues is for every believer. "And these signs will follow those who believe: In My name they will cast out demons; they will speak with new tongues" (Mk. 16:17). Today, if we proclaim the gospel and believe, then signs will follow, including speaking in tongues.

And they were all filled with the Holy Spirit and began to speak with other tongues, as the Spirit gave them utterance. And there were dwelling in Jerusalem Jews, devout men, from every nation under heaven. And when this sound occurred, the multitude came together, and were confused, because everyone heard them speak in his own language. Then they were all amazed and marveled, saying to one another, "Look, are not all these who speak Galileans? And how is it that we hear, each in our own language in which we were born? Parthians and Medes and Elamites, those dwelling in Mesopotamia, Judea and Cappadocia, Pontus and Asia, Phrygia and Pamphylia, Egypt and the parts of Libya adjoining Cyrene, visitors from Rome, both Jews and proselytes, Cretans and Arabs—we hear them speaking in our own tongues the wonderful works of God." So they were all amazed and perplexed, saying to one another, "Whatever could this mean?" (Acts 2:4-12).

On this occasion the manifestation of tongues was not for preaching the gospel so much as for praising God by praying in the Spirit.

Acts 10:44-46 says, "While Peter was still speaking these words, the Holy Spirit fell upon all those who heard the word. And those of the circumcision who believed were astonished, as many as came with Peter, because the gift of the Holy Spirit had been poured out on the Gentiles also. For they heard them speak with tongues and magnify God..." In this instance, which occurred in the house of Cornelius, a Roman centurion, the Holy Spirit fell on *all* who heard Peter speak, and they *all* began praising God in tongues.

*And it happened, while Apollos was at Corinth, that
Paul, having passed through the upper regions,
came to Ephesus. And finding some disciples he
said to them, "Did you receive the Holy Spirit when
you believed?" So they said to him, "We have not so
much as heard whether there is a Holy Spirit." And
he said to them, "Into what then were you baptized?" So they said, "Into John's baptism." Then
Paul said, "John indeed baptized with a baptism of
repentance, saying to the people that they should
believe on Him who would come after Him, that is,
on Christ Jesus." When they heard this, they were
baptized in the name of the Lord Jesus. And when
Paul had laid hands on them, the Holy Spirit came
upon them, and they spoke with tongues and prophesied. Now the men were about twelve in all* (Acts
19:1-7).

All twelve of the men upon whom Paul laid his hands to
impart the Holy Spirit began speaking in tongues. This spiritual gift is for all believers. Speaking in tongues is a scriptural way to praise God.

The Language of Men and Angels

Through the years I have witnessed many different effects
from speaking in tongues. Many years ago I ministered
in Czechoslovakia, and one of the phrases I learned was,
"Slava Bohu," which means "Glory to God!" Few Americans
will ever know that phrase or its meaning.

A few weeks later, I was ministering in San Antonio,
Texas. One of the men in attendance was a bona fide true blue
cowboy, decked out in his boots, jeans, and blue-checkered
shirt. He had come to the meeting as someone's guest, and

received Jesus as Savior that night. I said to him, "Now the Lord will baptize you in the Holy Spirit and give you a prayer language." Suddenly, the power of God hit this Texas cowboy. With his eyes wide open he raised his hands and began worshiping the Lord and speaking in perfect Czechoslovakian! Among the strange words, I heard him say "Slava Bohu!" many times. Upon further examination, I learned that this man was a third-generation Texan. Not only were he, his parents, and his grandparents all from Texas, he himself had never been outside the state! I knew that what was happening was real, because he truly was speaking in an unknown tongue.

Often, as we speak in tongues, it can be the language of men or the language of angels (see 1 Cor. 13:1).

Speaking in tongues is a sign for unbelievers. "Therefore tongues are for a sign, not to those who believe but to unbelievers; but prophesying is not for unbelievers but for those who believe" (1 Cor. 14:22). I remember once, while ministering in Ohio, a family from Israel accepted the Lord. They claimed that as I was preaching, I suddenly stopped and began speaking in Hebrew. Even though I do not claim to know Hebrew, apparently I began to call out each of these family members by name in Hebrew, telling them that they needed to receive Christ. They did receive Jesus as Savior and Lord and are now serving Him faithfully in Israel.

At one time, Bonnie and I did a lot of mission work in Africa. During one such occasion, although she had not been around the people long enough to learn their language, Bonnie had an amazing ability to speak to the women in their native Congo language of Lingala.

I know a little Swahili, but I cannot speak both Swahili and English at the same time. In just the same manner, I tell people after receiving Christ as Savior, "If you want to pray in tongues, don't speak in English anymore. Just open your mouth and the Holy Spirit will give you the words. By faith start speaking." We need to trust our heavenly Father. Remember, if we ask the Father, He will give good things. If we ask for the Holy Spirit, He will surely give us the Holy Spirit. Psalm 81:10 is a good Scripture to remember: "I am the Lord your God...open your mouth wide, and I will fill it."

When I started speaking in tongues, it wasn't like something beyond me came out and took control. I voluntarily opened my mouth and began to speak. The Holy Spirit gave the words, but I opened my mouth and spoke on my own volition. As it reads in Acts 2:4, "And they were all filled with the Holy Spirit and began to speak with other tongues, *as the Spirit gave them utterance.*"

My initial experience with tongues felt like tremendous, liquid love flowing all over me and through me. Sometimes people will feel a surge of emotions. This is a good indicator that God is coming in and healing inner hurts. I have seen people instantly receive healing from years of sexual and physical abuse or hurts they have been carrying for decades. As this healing begins to occur, often they will start to cry.

Strong emotion is not always present, however, because receiving is first of all an act of faith. Once people receive the prayer language of the Spirit, they can speak anytime they want to in English and anytime they want to in tongues. I don't have to wait on the Holy Spirit to move my tongue. It is just like speaking my regular language.

The Holy Spirit is like a living lamp illuminating our hearts. Our hearts are full of great secret chambers where He will come and shine His light. Where there has been death, darkness, and depression, light will start flooding in. Let it be according to God's Word. Let it be for God's excellent purposes in us and for us. Let it be God's purposes for our children. Let it be God's purposes for our ministry and calling. Let it be for God's purposes regarding His Church. Let it be!

There are several ways of praying in the Spirit in this heavenly language. One is personal edification where we individually pray, sing, worship, and magnify God. This can be considered our devotional language. Along with this is also a corporate lifting up of praise in speaking in tongues. This is like throwing love kisses up to Jesus together. We are communicating from our hearts. The most perfect praise we can give Him is in tongues. It is wonderful to have beautifully written and orchestrated songs, but the most awesome and perfect worship is speaking to Him in our heavenly language. I believe it's the bridal language and I believe in the last days, as the Lord pours out His Spirit, the Bride of Christ is going to come forth in the most awesome way and worship Him in spirit and in truth.

There is a difference between the devotional language and the gift of tongues mentioned in First Corinthians 14:5,13:"I wish you all spoke with tongues, but even more that you prophesied; for he who prophesies is greater than he who speaks with tongues, unless indeed he interprets, that the church may receive edification....Therefore let him who speaks in a tongue pray that he may interpret." The "tongues" in this passage refers to the gift of tongues manifested for congregational edification. It is exercised in a public manner with one voice speaking into the congregation first in a tongue and then giving the interpretation. Personal prayer language, on the other hand, is our speaking mysteries to God to edify ourselves.

In First Corinthians chapter 14, Paul spends an exceptional amount of time trying to clarify the confusion that was taking place in the Corinthian church over the matter of speaking in tongues. There were some in the congregation who would just shout out in tongues in public and cause confusion for unbelievers. This chapter is worthy of closer personal study by anyone seeking to understand about speaking in tongues. Paul was trying to establish some guidelines for the Corinthians to bring their practice into order, because God is not the author of confusion.

Bridal Language

Genesis chapter 24 tells of Rebekah, who is symbolic of the Bride of Christ, in the care of the chief steward, who is symbolic of the Holy Spirit. Just as the chief steward was responsible for bringing Rebekah home as a bride for Isaac, the Holy Spirit, the third Person of the Godhead, is responsible for preparing and bringing home the Bride of Christ. I believe the primary mode of communication between "Rebekah" and the "Chief Steward" is speaking in tongues.

I also believe that in the coming days there will be a greater emphasis on this bridal language. As we see the Bride emerge on the day of Pentecost, God makes her a citizen of Heaven and gives her the language of Heaven. All believers, therefore, who are part of the Bride, will have this language. We can remain mute if we wish and say nothing. That is our choice, but the language is available to us. It's a heavenly language, a bridal language.

The Holy Spirit is like the steward who came and searched for a bride for Isaac, found Rebekah, and took her home. The steward came to a far country to bring the bride home, and he wanted to communicate with her and tell her all about the bridegroom: what the bridegroom was like, what he desired for her to have, and how he wanted her to conduct herself. In the same way, the Holy Spirit wants to reveal the qualities and characteristics of the divine Bridegroom to the Bride. For example, all the covenant names of God rest in Jesus Christ our Bridegroom. For me, for example, *Jehovah Rapha* is an entire galaxy full of healing wonders. Then I go to the galaxy called *Jehovah Jireh*, the Lord our provider. How can I describe the multitude of wonders my spirit beholds? It is beyond the ability of my human language, even if I have the ability of Shakespeare. Jesus is beyond description. We need the tongue of angels. As we pray in tongues, His light, love, wisdom, and discernment are loosed in our lives.

The Holy Spirit is a wonderful witness. He helps in our weakness giving us wisdom and discernment. I remember while in graduate school I was still young in my spiritual walk. Only a few weeks after I came to the Lord, a person came to me wearing a big cross around his neck. I naturally assumed he was a Christian. I thought, "Oh, wonderful another Christian I can fellowship with." I was so hungry. After we approached one another and he started speaking to me, I felt the Holy Spirit inside saying "Warning! Warning! Warning!" I tried to argue. "But Lord, he's wearing this huge cross on his chest." The Holy Spirit insisted, "Warning! Warning! Warning!" This gentleman invited me to a meeting, but I decided not to attend due to my warning from the Holy Spirit. Later on I found out that he was in a cult called "The Children of God" that harmed many believers in the early days of the charismatic outpouring.

Here is my recommendation for those of you who want to get started in building up your faith by speaking in tongues. It's very simple. Pray in tongues as much as you can. If you have the time, pray for an hour, pray for five hours. I find personally, that I begin with about 30 minutes and suddenly I hit a spring of living water this brook. It begins to just bubble forth. This is where I begin building myself up in my most holy faith, praying in the Spirit. How much should I pray? The more you pray in tongues, the more you will feel like praying further. I believe at least thirty minutes is needed for us to prime the pump and prepare the way for an explosion in our spirit of joy unspeakable and full of glory. Begin to pray in tongues daily, even if it is only for fifteen minutes. Gradually increase the amount of time you pray in the spirit. If you pray in the spirit, the language of glory, faithfully and consistently for 40 days, you will see a big change in your life, a metamorphosis like that mentioned in Second Corinthians 3:17-18: "Now the Lord is the Spirit; and where the Spirit of the Lord *is*, there *is* liberty. But we all, with unveiled face, beholding as in a mirror the glory of the Lord, are being transformed into the same image from glory to glory, just as by the Spirit of the Lord." One thing is certain, after this time of praying in tongues you will be stronger in your spirit than you were before.

In a companion volume, *The Hidden Power of Prayer and Fasting*, I mentioned that besides carrying out my duties as a pastor, evangelist, parent and husband, I had extensive times of prayer and fasting. Any spare moment available I was in the Word, or praying primarily in tongues. Often there would be seasons where I would spend hours in the Lord's throne room praying in my heavenly language. During that time I found that while I was praying in tongues I was building myself up in "my most holy faith" according to Jude 1:20, "But you, beloved, building yourselves up on your most holy faith praying in the Holy Spirit."

We build ourselves up by praying in tongues. We are able to accomplish more than we could have ever hoped for in our own human capacity or strength. Ordinary people start accomplishing extraordinary things. Gideon became a deliverer; Joshua saw the defeat of Jericho; Samson slew hundreds of oppressing Philistines; young David slew the giant, Goliath; Elijah did great miracles, and Elisha doubled them; Peter lost his fear and boldly preached on Pentecost, and Paul raised the dead. The list goes on. What was the key to accomplishing extraordinary exploits in all these heroes of faith? In every case it was the same thing: Holy Spirit empowerment. "'Not by might nor by power but by My Spirit,' Says the Lord of hosts" (Zech. 4:6). Jesus was the culmination: "God anointed Jesus of Nazareth with the Holy Spirit and with power, who went about doing good and healing all who were oppressed by the devil, for God was with Him" (Acts 10:38).

All of these spiritual principles can be combined in our lives by watching and praying. It has been our privilege to lead a global prayer movement called The Watch of the Lord™. As we have consistently watched and prayed these last eight years for many hours on Friday nights, an anointed pattern has emerged. At the beginning of the evening we praise and worship for several hours. Afterwards, we participate in a prayer wheel, walking corporately and confessing the Word out loud, and then we often pray in tongues together. This is a pattern that you can also use as a model in your individual life. I also suggest that those who receive the baptism of the Holy Spirit become active members of a local church, honoring the pastors of the congregation. It is wise to choose a congregation which welcomes the move of the Holy Spirit. Find an anointed pastor who can further guide you in your spiritual journey.

Chapter Four

BAPTIZED IN THE SPIRIT

In 1999 and the early days of 2000, interest in the millennium reached fever pitch worldwide. Millennial fever spread like an epidemic as people watched and waited, in varied degrees of anxiety, to see whether the so-called Y2K bug would take down the computer systems of the world and thrust human civilization back into a technological stone age. Many Christians throughout the world also watched to see what the arrival of the new millennium might mean with regard to the Church, Israel, biblical prophecy, the return of Christ, and the end of the world.

Although Y2K turned out to be pretty much a non-event, the arrival of the new millennium does represent for humanity new opportunities and new challenges. The Christian Church, which historically has often been slow to respond, must rise to these new opportunities and challenges or risk losing its prophetic voice before the world. At the same time, we must never change or dilute our message. New opportunities and challenges call for new methods, not a new message. Our gospel message never changes—"Jesus Christ and Him crucified" is fundamental and central—but our methods of proclaiming that message must change to meet new demands. Within biblical parameters, we must broaden our horizons and look to God to do *new things* as well as to do *old things in new ways.*

Ecclesiastes 1:9b says "there is nothing new under the sun." That may be true from mankind's perspective, but God does not look at things from our point of view. He has said, "Do not remember the former things, nor consider the things of old. Behold, I will do a new thing, now it shall spring forth; shall you not know it? I will even make a road in the wilderness and rivers in the desert" (Is. 43:18-19). God is always doing new things—He is a God of the new—and the new things He does will always be in line with what He has done in the past, both in spirit and in purpose, because God never changes.

At the dawn of the twentieth century God did a new thing when, in the early hours of January 1, 1901, the Holy Spirit came upon a group of seeking students at a Christian academy in Topeka, Kansas, led by a minister named Charles Parham. In a manifestation rarely seen since the first century, these students began to speak in tongues. Five years later William Seymour, a black preacher who had been deeply influenced by the Topeka experience, was present when the Spirit fell again, this time in a black ghetto in Los Angeles, at an old warehouse on Azuza Street. Once again, the Holy Spirit came with the evidence of speaking in tongues.

From these small beginnings the modern Pentecostal movement was born, growing steadily and inexorably until, at the dawn of the twenty-first century and the third millennium since Christ, the Pentecostal/Charismatic branch is the fastest growing wing in the Christian Church. Today, over half of all evangelical Christians claim the "baptism of the Holy Spirit" with the accompanying evidence of speaking in tongues, and the numbers are still growing with no end in sight. In these last days, clearly, God is doing a new thing.

What does this mean then for the Church in the twenty-first century? What will be the significance of the "baptism of the Holy Spirit" for the Church entering the new millennium? Will the Holy Spirit continue to be a point of division among believers, as so often in the past, or will He become a rallying point of unity for the Body of Christ, bringing us together as never before and empowering us to meet the unique challenges that lie ahead as we seek to prepare the world for Christ's return?

The Holy Spirit: Point of Division or Agent of Unity?

I am convinced that in the twenty-first century the Holy Spirit's role in the life and ministry of the Church will be even greater, more powerful, and more fundamental than in the century we have just left behind. Accordingly, the baptism of the Holy Spirit also will assume greater significance than in the past. Our generation or that of our children may well be the one to witness the bodily return of Jesus Christ to earth and the end of this present age. Because of this, the Christian Church even now may be entering the most significant period of its history.

As the light of the gospel shines brighter and brighter throughout the world, the powers of darkness will rise in ever-increasing ferocity to oppose it. Since the days of Jesus Himself, the spirit of antichrist also has been loose in the world. Any spirit, teaching, religion, or philosophy that denies Jesus Christ serves the spirit of antichrist. John the apostle wrote, "Every spirit that does not confess that Jesus Christ has come in the flesh is not of God. And this is the spirit of the antichrist, which you have heard was coming, and is now already in the world" (1 Jn. 4:3).

Today in our world the spirit of antichrist is revealing itself continually in new and more insidious forms. One of the most visible of these is the rise of radical, militant Islamic fundamentalism of the type that inspires ongoing violence against Israel and which lies behind the September 11, 2001 terrorist attacks on the World Trade Center in New York City and on the Pentagon in our nation's capital. Such a movement as this exemplifies the spirit of antichrist because of its hatred for the God of the Bible. It hates the Son of God, the people of God, and everything they stand for.

In the face of this and similar threats, the Church, which exemplifies the Spirit of Christ, cannot afford to be divided, yet that is just where we find ourselves. One of satan's primary strategies all along in his war against Christ's Church has been "divide and conquer," and he is very good at it. As long as he can keep us disagreeing and fighting among ourselves, he can prevent us from forming a united front against him and his schemes.

Ironically enough, one of the greatest points of controversy and division in the Church, at least for the last 100 years or so, has centered on the question of the role and ministry of the Holy Spirit and, in particular, the nature and meaning of the "baptism of the Holy Spirit." How sad it is that we have allowed ourselves to become so divided over the One who was given to the Church as an agent of unity. For far too long we have allowed the Holy Spirit to become a point of religious or doctrinal dispute that separates us, when all along His purpose is to unite us in Christ. Paul considered the issue important enough to give these instructions to the believers of the church in Ephesus:

> *I, therefore, the prisoner of the Lord, beseech you*
> *to walk worthy of the calling with which you were*

called, with all lowliness and gentleness, with longsuffering, bearing with one another in love, endeavoring to keep the unity of the Spirit in the bond of peace. There is one body and one Spirit, just as you were called in one hope of your calling; one Lord, one faith, one baptism; one God and Father of all, who is above all, and through all, and in you all (Ephesians 4:1-6).

He addressed the same theme with the Corinthians:

For as the body is one and has many members, but all the members of that one body, being many, are one body, so also is Christ. For by one Spirit we were all baptized into one body—whether Jews or Greeks, whether slaves or free—and have all been made to drink into one Spirit. For in fact the body is not one member but many (1 Corinthians 12:12-14).

Throughout the New Testament, the presence of the Holy Spirit is closely associated with unity among believers. Much of our modern controversy and division over the Holy Spirit has to do with the character of His presence and work in us and the nature of the "baptism" through which He fills and empowers us. It is this "baptism of the Holy Spirit" that we need to understand.

For the sake of clarity and understanding, I want to state plainly that I believe in the baptism of the Holy Spirit as a *separate* act of God's grace apart from but in conjunction with salvation, although it frequently occurs at the same time. *All* believers receive the Holy Spirit as the agent of regeneration when they first come to Christ, and He takes up permanent residence in their hearts. Based on my own experience and that of many other dear believers and friends whom I know, as well as the witness of nearly 30 years of ministry in the United

States and around the world, I believe that there is another "receiving" of the Spirit available to believers, a "receiving" or a "baptism" of the Holy Spirit, not for salvation, but for *power* in ministry.

I realize that there are many sincere and committed believers who love Jesus who will take issue with me at this very point. It is not my desire or intent to throw down a gauntlet of challenge at the feet of any of my brothers or sisters in Christ, particularly those who disagree with me on this matter. We have too much in common to let this divide us, and too much work to do to allow it to sunder our fellowship with one another. The central issue is Jesus Christ. Anyone who can affirm with me that "Jesus Christ is Lord," and that the heart and soul of our message is "Jesus Christ, and Him crucified," is my brother or sister in Christ. These affirmations give us the common bond of faith that we need in order to fellowship together and work together to advance the Kingdom of our Lord.

With matters of the Spirit, as with anything else, we must examine all things by the unchanging standard of God's Word. Even the Bible, however, leaves room for God to do the unexpected. The four Gospels, and particularly the Gospel of John, make it clear that not everything that Jesus said or did was recorded. Not every sign or wonder or work that He performed was written down. This should allow us some flexibility when deciding whether or not something "new" that is happening is of God. Even if something is not explicitly stated in Scripture, if it falls into the pattern of that which Scripture affirms, and in no way violates the express teaching of Scripture, we are usually safe in embracing it as a work of God, even if it is new to our own experience.

I want to discuss the baptism of the Holy Spirit from my perspective—what it is and what it means—not as a gauntlet of challenge or an instrument of division, but as an invitation to reexamine this wonderful *gift* of the Lord, His power for His Church in every generation, and especially as we enter the new millennium.

Rivers of Living Water

Once, when the apostle Paul was in the city of Ephesus, he met some disciples, whom he asked, "Did you receive the Holy Spirit when you believed?" (Acts 19:2a) Upon their reply that they had never heard of the Holy Spirit, Paul probed further and discovered that they were disciples of John the Baptist, having received John's baptism in water for repentance and the forgiveness of sins. Paul then told them about Jesus, the One to whom John had given witness as the Son of God.

> *When they heard this, they were baptized in the name of the Lord Jesus. And when Paul had laid hands on them, the Holy Spirit came upon them, and they spoke with tongues and prophesied. Now the men were about twelve in all* (Acts 19:5-7).

In a way, I as a young believer was like those disciples of John. I was born in Africa to Indian parents. When I first came to Christ, I was genuinely born again and was baptized publicly in the Indian Ocean. Even facing the threat of persecution, I wanted to follow the Lord faithfully, but at that time no one taught me about the significance of the Holy Spirit to my Christian life. No one told me about the strength and power of the Spirit that were available to help me grow strong in faith and ministry.

Some years later, when I was just entering graduate school in the United States, I received the news that my mother, who was living in England, was dying of a terminal illness. I did not have the money to go see her. A great cloud of depression came over me, and I heard voices inside telling me that I was a failure. I was a big nothing because I couldn't even visit my mother when she needed me the most. Emotionally distraught over my mother's illness, I readily agreed with these inner voices. Then they began to say, "You know, it would be better if you just ended it now. End it now. End it now."

Today, of course, I recognize that this was the devil trying to thwart the destiny and purpose that God had for my life. That night, however, I was in deep distress and began to pray; there was nothing else I could do. To my surprise, the Lord Himself came and baptized me in His Holy Spirit. I was bubbling in tongues and for hours could not stop singing in the Spirit. At the same time, the Spirit drove out of me three demon spirits of death, depression, and suicide. On top of it all, the Lord miraculously healed my mother and she lived for another 20 years.

Although I did not realize it at the time, I was experiencing personally the "rivers of living water" that Jesus Himself promised in John 7:

> *On the last day, that great day of the feast, Jesus stood and cried out, saying, "If anyone thirsts, let him come to Me and drink. He who believes in Me, as the Scripture has said, out of his heart will flow rivers of living water." But this He spoke concerning the Spirit, whom those believing in Him would receive; for the Holy Spirit was not yet given, because Jesus was not yet glorified* (John 7:37-39).

The setting was Jerusalem during the Feast of Tabernacles, a great eight-day festival characterized by joy and celebration, which commemorated Israel's journey in the wilderness from Egypt to Canaan and celebrated God's presence with His people. One of the significant characteristics of the feast was the daily processional of the priests carrying a pitcher of water from the pool of Siloam to pour out at the base of the altar in the Temple. Although it is uncertain whether this processional normally occurred on the eighth and final day of the feast, it was on that day that Jesus extended His powerful invitation.

Jesus "cried out" to the people and spoke to them of "rivers of living water." John explains that Jesus' words referred to the Holy Spirit, who would come after Jesus was glorified. That promise was fulfilled on the day of Pentecost.

The coming of the Holy Spirit at Pentecost revolutionized the Church, even at its very beginning, transforming it from a small, weak, insignificant group into a powerhouse of faith, signs, and wonders that transformed its culture and environment within two generations. I believe that in our day the Lord wants to revolutionize His Church again, not only in the corporate sense, but within our individual lives as well. As on the day of Pentecost, the instrument of that revolution is the Holy Spirit.

For the last 1900 years, with a few exceptions, the Church for the most part has not fully recognized who the Holy Spirit is or fully acknowledged His importance in its life and mission. Jesus' death accomplished two things for us. First, His shed blood made it possible for us to be saved and brought into a right relationship with God. Second, His departure opened the way for the coming of the Holy Spirit. What a wonderful, absolutely awesome gift Jesus gave to us when He gave us His

Spirit! The living presence of the Lord abiding in our hearts is more precious than anything earth could ever offer us. As it says in Proverbs:

> *Happy is the man who finds wisdom, And the man who gains understanding; for her proceeds are better than the profits of silver, And her gain than fine gold. She is more precious than rubies, And all the things you may desire cannot compare with her* (Proverbs 3:13-15).

Although the passage is speaking specifically about wisdom, it is with the understanding that God is the source of wisdom. From our perspective as followers of Christ, this equates to the Holy Spirit, who gives us the wisdom of God, who teaches us all things, and brings to our remembrance everything that Jesus said (see Jn. 14:26). The living presence of the Holy Spirit in our hearts makes all of us who are believers the richest people on earth.

Quenching Our Spiritual Thirst

In John 7:37-38 Jesus invited all who were thirsty to come to Him and drink and promised that all who believed in Him would have their hearts flowing with "rivers of living water." Every human being, without exception, has that spiritual thirst, although millions are not consciously aware of it. Just as our physical bodies need water every day to survive, so our spirits need the life-giving spiritual water of the Holy Spirit every day in order to thrive. The more water we drink, the healthier we are physically. By the same token, the more of the Holy Spirit we "drink," the healthier we are spiritually. The baptism of the Holy Spirit enables us to drink freely of the Spirit, not just tiny sips but great draughts of refreshing living water.

After only three days without water the human body begins to shut down and approaches death. In the same way, people all around us are dying without the supernatural water of the Holy Spirit. Jesus said, "If anyone thirsts, let him come to Me and drink." That is a very simple invitation, yet there are so many people who do not accept it simply because they do not know that they are thirsty.

People who do not know Jesus do not turn to Him because satan keeps them in the dark by confusing their minds. He diverts their attention from their true spiritual thirst by drawing them into the occult, New Age, or Eastern religions, and by seducing them with false promises of happiness through materialism and the pursuit of riches. All of these may appear at first to quench thirst but prove in the end to be dry wells.

Unfortunately, there are many Christian believers as well who have rarely if ever experienced their hearts flowing with "rivers of living water." Their sense of thirst has been dulled either by ignorance of the Holy Spirit or by doctrines or teachings that insist that the gifts and fullness of the Holy Spirit are not available for believers today.

The only way to quench our spiritual thirst is with daily draughts of the Holy Spirit. We need to "drink" of the Spirit every day. Jesus did not promise us a glass of water if we came to Him, but rivers of living water. He is so generous, giving freely and liberally to all who humbly seek Him.

Speaking in tongues is one of the best tools available to us for drinking of the Spirit. It helps us become clear and open "tributaries" for the rivers of living water. Tongues opens the door not only for us to receive God's blessings but to be His instruments in blessing others as well. In my own life and experience I have discovered a major key to success that I readily recommend to other believers. It is simply this: Commit yourself to pray in tongues for 30 minutes every day and see how much your life will change over the next year. This is not a magic formula, but a spiritual endowment that releases the water of the Spirit to flow in and through our lives.

The Holy Spirit is the administrator of all the gifts and treasures of God and He makes all the resources of the Kingdom of Heaven available to believers. He holds the key that opens the door to the Lord's blessings, and says to us, "Okay, go on in and get whatever you want." As followers of Christ we are children of God and all the treasuries of glory belong to us.

The Language of the Spirit

If the Holy Spirit administrates the gifts of God, then the baptism of the Holy Spirit gives us access to them. First Corinthians 12:11b says that the Holy Spirit distributes spiritual gifts "to each one individually as He wills." One of those gifts is tongues. The Gospels of Luke and John, as well as the Book of Acts, link the Holy Spirit with the provision of wisdom, understanding, and power to believers. The Book of Acts also clearly associates the baptism of the Holy Spirit with the outward manifestation of speaking in tongues. Whenever direct reference is made to the baptism of the Holy Spirit, that baptism is accompanied and signified by speaking in tongues on the part of those who have just received the Spirit.

Speaking in tongues was such an integral part of the Pentecost experience that to attempt to deny or play down its significance is to destroy much of the meaning of that event. Because it represents the presence of the Holy Spirit, taking tongues out of Pentecost removes its spiritual backbone, leaving "a form of godliness but denying its power" (2 Tim. 3:5a).

The baptism of the Holy Spirit releases in us the grace of speaking in tongues, which is the language of the Spirit. It is the language that we as the Bride of Christ can use in speaking to our Bridegroom and which He can speak to us—two-way communication at a much deeper level than human language is capable of. It is similar to that which the psalmist described when he wrote, "Deep calls unto deep at the noise of Your waterfalls; all Your waves and billows have gone over me" (Ps. 42:7). Speaking in tongues is an expression of love and communion producing an intimacy with the Lord that is too deep for human words.

By its very nature, tongues is endowed with intercessory power. Like the Navajo "windtalkers" of World War II, whenever we speak or pray in tongues we make use of an unbreakable code that excludes and frustrates our enemy, the devil, in all of His schemes. Speaking in tongues is like installing a "firewall" on our spiritual computer: It prevents satan from "hacking" into our system to infect it with his "virus" of evil and corruption.

Just as the computer revolutionized and transformed the face and fabric of modern society in less than one generation, I believe the baptism of the Holy Spirit will revolutionize and transform the face and fabric of the Church during the first generation of the new millennium. Today we have learned to "speak" an electronic language that was unknown 50 years ago. In the same manner, more and more believers will learn a new spiritual language that will prepare and equip them for Kingdom work in the new millennium.

Compass and Needle

Another significant value of the baptism of the Holy Spirit is that it helps give us stable and reliable direction for our lives. For centuries sailors, explorers, armies, and other travelers have depended on a simple device to show them the right way to go: the magnetic compass. Even earlier, before the age of the compass, men learned to determine their position and direction in reference to Polaris, also known as the North Star. Both of these methods involve using north as a fixed reference point from which position and desired direction may then be determined.

As long as the proper conditions prevail, a compass and the North Star are reliable guides. A cloudy night, however, will shroud Polaris from view, and any magnetized material brought close enough to a compass will cause it to give an incorrect reading.

All of us need a reliable "compass" to help us determine our direction in life. Where are we going? How are we going to get there? Which way do we turn? How do we know which path to take?

Fortunately, God has provided us with such a compass: His Word. The Bible is our spiritual compass that will help us find our way, keep us from getting lost, and point us to our fixed reference point—truth. If the Bible is our compass, the Holy Spirit is the needle that always directs us to "true north." The Scriptures relate north to the dwelling place of God, to His very presence and Person:

> *Great is the Lord, and greatly to be praised in the city of our God, in His holy mountain. Beautiful in elevation, the joy of the whole earth, is Mount Zion on the sides of the north, the city of the great King* (Psalm 48:1-2).

In another sense, Jesus Himself is "true north," because it is to Him that the Holy Spirit points us always. True north never changes, and neither does Jesus. He is reliable and steadfast, "the same yesterday, today, and forever" (Heb. 13:8). If we trust and follow the Holy Spirit, He will lead us unerringly in the footsteps of Jesus and into our full destiny as children of God. "For as many as are led by the Spirit of God, these are sons of God" (Rom. 8:14).

God has two specific purposes in mind for each of us: to deliver us and to direct us. He sent His Son, Jesus Christ, to earth to accomplish the first through His death on the cross and His resurrection. To accomplish the second, He sent the Holy Spirit to dwell in the hearts of all who place their faith and trust in Jesus. The directions He has given us to follow are so basic and simple that even a child can understand them:

> ...*You shall love the Lord your God with all your heart, with all your soul, and with all your mind* (Matthew 22:37).

> *Go therefore and make disciples of all the nations, baptizing them in the name of the Father and of the Son and of the Holy Spirit, teaching them to observe all things that I have commanded you* (Matthew 28:19-20a).

> ...*Go into all the world and preach the gospel to every creature* (Mark 16:15).

> *But you shall receive power when the Holy Spirit has come upon you; and you shall be witnesses to Me in Jerusalem, and in all Judea and Samaria, and to the end of the earth* (Acts 1:8).

God saved and delivered us that we might love and serve Him. The Spirit of God always leads us in that direction; He keeps us always facing and following God. It does not matter what others say or think. We must keep our eyes fixed on

Jesus. If we turn aside from Him to listen to someone else, we will get lost.

The Holy Spirit is our Guide. He is so faithful. As we trust the Spirit's guidance, as we pray, and as we speak in tongues, He will not let us lose direction. His purpose is to prepare us and deliver us safe and sound into the hands of our Bridegroom. Just as the Holy Spirit helped Jesus stay the course during His earthly life, so He will help us stay the course on our journey. The Holy Spirit is the needle in our spiritual compass, and if we follow Him faithfully, we will find ourselves safely home in the arms of Jesus.

Power and Unity

Jesus promised that His followers would receive power when the Holy Spirit came upon them, and that power would enable them to be His witnesses throughout the world. A corollary to this that is often overlooked because it is not directly stated is that with the *power* of the Spirit comes the *unity* of the Spirit. Divided or unfocused power often dissipates quickly, wasting much valuable energy. A divided Church will have a hard time fulfilling the Great Commission. Through the Holy Spirit, the Body of Christ has been given tremendous power, but we must be united in purpose and fellowship if we are to exercise our power to its fullest effect. The same Holy Spirit who gives us power wants to bring us to unity.

That is the pattern of Pentecost. The Spirit came with power and united the 120 believers in that upper room. They began to speak in tongues and went out into the streets where people from every part of the Roman Empire heard the gospel in their own language. Through the power of the Spirit, 3,000 of them came to Christ that day and that same Spirit brought them into unity with the other believers.

> *And they continued steadfastly in the apostles' doctrine and fellowship, in the breaking of bread, and in prayers....Now all who believed were together, and had all things in common, and sold their possessions and goods, and divided them among all, as anyone had need. So continuing daily with one accord in the temple, and breaking bread from house to house, they ate their food with gladness and simplicity of heart* (Acts 2:42,44-46).

The baptism of the Holy Spirit is not only a baptism of power, but also a baptism of unity. In the work of God's Kingdom, power and unity go together. Where the Spirit of God holds sway, the people of God dwell in peace and one accord.

The Spirit-baptized Church of the new millennium will be increasingly characterized by the removal of dividing walls—traditional barriers of race, culture, and socio-economic status. "There is neither Jew nor Greek, there is neither slave nor free, there is neither male nor female; for you are all one in Christ Jesus" (Gal. 3:28). "There is neither Greek nor Jew, circumcised nor uncircumcised, barbarian, Scythian, slave nor free, but Christ is all and in all" (Col. 3:11). Rather than thinking in terms of "white" churches, "black" churches, "Hispanic" churches, "rich" churches, "poor" churches, "high" churches, or "low" churches, we will see ourselves truly as *one* body in Christ, *one* family in the Lord.

Although certain doctrinal and theological distinctions between individuals or groups undoubtedly will remain, the influence of the Holy Spirit will create a general environment of unity amidst diversity: unity in essentials, diversity in nonessentials. The essentials are those central and fundamental truths upon which the Christian faith rests: the absolute authority and integrity of God's Word as our standard for everything; personal repentance of sin and faith in and devotion to Jesus Christ; the unchanging bedrock message of Jesus Christ crucified, buried, risen, and returning; and dependence on the Holy Spirit for power in daily living and ministry. The nonessentials are everything else.

As believers we have a commission from Christ, a responsibility to proclaim the gospel and make disciples in every nation and help set the stage for the return of Jesus and the establishment of His ruler over all the earth. "And this gospel of the kingdom will be preached in all the world as a witness to all the nations, and then the end will come" (Mt. 24:14). The Holy Spirit gives us both the power to proclaim the gospel with authority and the unity to live that gospel daily as credible witnesses before a spiritually hungry but skeptical world.

This is the same gospel of the Kingdom that Jesus preached and taught His disciples to preach. It is the same gospel that they preached fearlessly in the Book of Acts, a gospel of power that changed lives. It is a gospel that I call the "full gospel" because it was the Word of God proclaimed in spiritual power with signs and wonders accompanying. Jesus preached *and* performed signs and wonders; so did the apostles and others in the Book of Acts. I believe this "full gospel" is for today as much as it was for the first century, based both on the example of the New Testament Church and on Christ's promise in the Gospel of Mark:

> ...*Go into all the world and preach the gospel to every creature. He who believes and is baptized will be saved; but he who does not believe will be condemned. And these signs will follow those who believe: In My name they will cast out demons; they will*

speak with new tongues; they will take up serpents;
and if they drink anything deadly, it will by no
means hurt them; they will lay hands on the sick,
and they will recover (Mark 16:15-18).

The baptism of the Holy Spirit draws us into the supernatural realm of signs and wonders. Flowing in the Spirit's power we can preach with authority, cast out demons, heal the sick, and through speaking in tongues, pray in the language of Heaven. If we desire to walk in the way of the Holy Spirit, we cannot be halfhearted or noncommittal; we must be prepared to be *changed*. Holy Spirit baptism brings transformation. He gives us a new heart, a new outlook, a new attitude, and a new language, and teaches us to have the mind of Christ.

Baptism in the Holy Spirit is the conduit or pipeline for the power of effective living. Speaking in tongues is the key that unlocks that power, the "superconductor" that speeds its passage through the pipeline. It is the bridal language of the Bride of Christ.

Chapter Five

BRIDAL LANGUAGE BENEFITS

The bridal language of Christ releases life-changing benefits for every believer. I will never forget a time in Houston one Sunday morning when about 50 children confessed Christ and received the Holy Spirit. While they were praying softly in their new prayer language, a little Mexican boy about six years old started shouting in his new tongue. As he carried on in a loud voice I, lacking understanding or discernment on what was happening, tried to calm him down. It didn't work. He continued to pray loudly in tongues.

About fifteen minutes later I heard a cry from the back. A tall Mexican gentleman rushed forward weeping, hugged his little son, and gave his life to the Lord. This man had turned away from his family. His little son was praying through in the Spirit for his father, not knowing he was standing in the back of the auditorium. The dark cloud lifted from the father, who that day received Christ. Like his son, He received the infilling of the Spirit with tongues and later was reconciled with his family.

When we ask Christ into our heart, we become new creations in Christ. "Therefore, if anyone is in Christ, he is a new creation; old things have passed away; behold, all things have become new" (2 Cor. 5:17). Most of us, however, still carry in our heart pictures of the past: shadows of rejections, fears, and wounds from the past. Even though we may desire to sing a new song of joy, often it is the old records of gloom and failure that begin playing again. God wants to come in and break those hurtful records.

Immediately after receiving the new birth experience, believers in the New Testament started speaking in new tongues. A fearful, motley crew became a dynamic army, boldly proclaiming the gospel with signs and wonders. I see tongues as a powerful force helping to erase the images of past hurts, failures, and fears.

Speaking in tongues carries enormous and valuable benefits for believers. Let's look at some of them.

1. When we speak in tongues we keep a commandment of the Lord.

> *What is the conclusion then? I will pray with the spirit, and I will also pray with the understanding. I will sing with the spirit, and I will also sing with the understanding....let him acknowledge that the things which I write to you are the commandments of the Lord* (First Corinthians 14:15,37).

2. When we speak in tongues we spiritual build an edifice of faith for our lives. I would ask every believer: Is your structure a skyscraper or a shack? If you feel your structure is small, there is a God-given plan for how you can build yourself up and add on to your faith. In its place, tongues assists the building up of a wonderful edifice of faith, pictures in our heart of victory in Christ.

> *He who speaks in a tongue edifies himself, but he who prophesies edifies the church* (1 Corinthians 14:4).

But you, beloved, building yourselves up on your most holy faith, praying in the Holy Spirit (Jude 1:20).

Keep your heart with all diligence, For out of it spring the issues of life (Proverbs 4:23).

3. When we speak in tongues we walk in obedience to the Lord and experience more of the power of His Spirit while fulfilling His great commission.

And these signs will follow those who believe: In My name they will cast out demons; they will speak with new tongues...they shall lay hands on the sick and they shall recover (Mark 16:17-18).

4. Our prayer language calls forth the secret truths and hidden things only known in the intimate places of Heaven.

For he who speaks in a tongue does not speak to men but to God, for no one understands him; however, in the spirit he speaks mysteries (1 Corinthians 14:2).

For one who speaks in an [unknown] tongue speaks not to men but to God, for no one understands or catches his meaning, because in the [Holy] Spirit he utters secret truths and hidden things [not obvious to the understanding] (1 Corinthians 14:2 AMP).

5. When we speak in tongues we convey the glorious acts of God.

We hear them speaking in our own tongues the wonderful works of God (Acts 2:11b).

6. When we speak in tongues it is a literal "jump-start" in the Spirit activating an explosion of faith into every area of our life.

Over the years we have experienced tremendous miracles in our ministry. Whenever I confront a faith challenge in my life, I immediately and quickly start speaking in tongues. It is my mustard seed release of faith for every challenging situation.

But you, beloved, building yourselves up on your most holy faith, praying in the Holy Spirit (Jude 1:20).

7. Whenever we speak in tongues, we offer perfect prayer to the Lord. Because we are in perfect agreement with the Lord, we are able to break through the heavenlies and reach the throne of God. The Message paraphrase of Scripture eloquently states how the Holy Spirit relieves us of our burden as we bare our heart concerns before the Lord.

God's Spirit touches our spirits and confirms who we really are. We know who he is, and we know who we are: Father and children. And we know we are going to get what's coming to us—an unbelievable inheritance! (Romans 8:16-17 The Message).

8. When we speak in tongues we pray for things beyond our knowledge and comprehension. It takes us beyond our intellectual capacity and out of the grasp of the natural realm. The more we realize that we need to get our analytical mindset off its throne, the more Jesus will be enthroned in our lives. Within that glory of the enthroned King is an atmosphere pregnant with miracles that will astound us all.

Likewise the Spirit also helps in our weaknesses. For we do not know what we should pray for as we ought, but the Spirit Himself makes intercession for us with groanings which cannot be uttered (Romans 8:26).

9. Speaking in tongues causes our spirit to stand side by side with the Holy Spirit, laying hold of all the promises of God regarding our inheritance in Christ Jesus. Using our prayer language we validate the claim of our inheritance as a child of God.

> *The Spirit Himself bears witness with our spirit that we are children of God. And if children, then heirs; heirs of God and joint heirs with Christ, if indeed we suffer with Him, that we may also be glorified together* (Romans 8:16-17).

10. Speaking in tongues is a holy instrument given by God for rest and refreshing to all believers to circumvent the effects of weariness and stress.

> *For with stammering lips and another tongue He will speak to this people, to whom He said, "This is the rest with which You may cause the weary to rest," And, "This is the refreshing"; yet they would not hear* (Isaiah 28:11-12).

11. Like an athlete training for a race, speaking in tongues causes our inner man to be toned and invigorated for the race set before us.

> *...that He would grant you, according to the riches of His glory, to be strengthened with might through His Spirit in the inner man* (Ephesians 3:16).

12. This love language of the Bride can woo those who don't know Christ and cause them to believe.

> *Therefore tongues are for a sign, not to those who believe but to unbelievers; but prophesying is not*

for unbelievers but for those who believe (1 Corinthians 14:22).

*And these signs will follow those who believe: In My
name they will cast out demons; they will speak
with new tongues* (Mark 16:17).

**13. As I pray in the spirit it is a compass in my life
pointing true North, always assuring me of the Lord's presence through every challenge.**

*And those of the circumcision who believed were
astonished, as many as came with Peter, because the
gift of the Holy Spirit had been poured out on the
Gentiles also. For they heard them speak with
tongues and magnify God* (Acts 10:45-46).

**14. Exercising my prayer language releases the
essence of wisdom, guidance, and discernment.**

*For he who speaks in a tongue does not speak to
men but to God, for no one understands him; however, in the spirit he speaks mysteries* (1 Corinthians
14:2).

*But we speak the wisdom of God in a mystery, the
hidden wisdom which God ordained before the ages
for our glory* (1 Corinthians 2:7).

**15. There is an ease in thanksgiving and a heartfelt
rejoicing as we proclaim the goodness of God in this heavenly language.** Ephesians 5:19 says, "speaking to one another...singing and making melody in your heart to the Lord,
giving thanks always..." The Bride should always be in this
atmosphere of harmony and thanksgiving. A heart of murmur-
ing, complaining, and unthankfulness will stop the supernatural flow of the river of God. Whenever I see that happen to
someone, I tell him or her, "You are stuck in the river." The

best way to get unstuck is to let the water rise through aggressive prayer in the Spirit and through worship and praise. Ephesians 5:18 is a divine prescription: "And do not be drunk with wine, in which is dissipation; but be filled with the Spirit..." When we are filled with the Spirit people often will think we are inebriated because the more we soak in the presence of the Holy Spirit the more joyful we will become.

Most major civilizations throughout history began around river basins. In the natural, wherever rivers are, life blossoms, commerce expands, and agriculture grows. In the spiritual realm, as we pray in the spirit, the river of God starts bubbling out resulting in life, healing, restoration, and provision.

> ...in everything give thanks; for this is the will of God in Christ Jesus for you (1 Thessalonians 5:18).

> Enter into His gates with thanksgiving, and into His courts with praise. Be thankful to Him, and bless His name (Psalm 100:4).

16. When we speak in tongues, allowing the Holy Spirit to take charge, our tongue is brought under God's control. Other areas of our lives that are in disarray will be brought into alignment with God's Word.

> But no man can tame the tongue. It is an unruly evil, full of deadly poison (James 3:8).

> ...that if you confess with your mouth the Lord Jesus and believe in your heart that God has raised Him from the dead, you will be saved (Romans 10:9).

I recall leading a pastor's seminar in another state on the gifts of the Spirit, where several hundred pastors attended. After the morning session, about 150 of us went to a very large restaurant for lunch. With that many ministers together in one place, the noise level was quite high. It seemed as though everyone needed something from the waitress.

I calmed myself by praying softly in tongues, and an ocean of peace seemed to surround me. My eyes fell on one harried waitress who was trying hard to keep up with the many demands of such a large crowd. Suddenly, in my spirit I started seeing a picture of a five-year-old boy on a kidney dialysis machine. As I prayed in the Spirit some more I suddenly realized the picture was connected with the young waitress. I waited to see if any of the other pastors would say anything to her regarding her need. No one talked with her except about his or her food order.

At the conclusion of the lunch I called the waitress over. She appeared nervous, perhaps expecting some kind of rebuke. I took her hand and said, "I have never met you but the Lord shows me that you are a single mother with a five-year-old son critically ill with kidney failure. The doctors have given a poor prognosis." She started to cry and asked, "Who are you?" I replied, "I am simply a servant of God." She kept crying saying, "My little boy is dying." I said, "I believe the reason I got this supernatural word is that the Lord is going to heal your son." She wept and thanked me.

The picture the Lord gave me as I prayed in the Spirit that day was 100 percent true, and once again the Holy Spirit ministered the mercy of Jesus. The gift of the Spirit we have been talking about here is to comfort, bless, and heal a hurting world. The anointing has come to heal the brokenhearted and give good news to the poor (see Luke 4:18).

This example illustrates one of the greatest values of speaking in tongues: it puts us in a place of being able to hear and understand the voice of the Lord.

Chapter Six

THE VOICE OF THE LORD

Acts 1:4 refers to the Holy Spirit as "the Promise of the Father," a promise that was fulfilled on the day of Pentecost when the Holy Spirit was poured out on the 120 believers who were gathered in that upper room in Jerusalem (see Acts 2:1-4). In Romans 8:23 the apostle Paul mentions the "first-fruits of the Spirit" as the common possession of all believers.

Mosaic Law specified three annual feasts that all Jews were required to observe. The first of these was Passover, which commemorated Israel's deliverance from slavery in Egypt and therefore represents our salvation. Second was the Feast of Pentecost, followed later in the year by the Feast of Tabernacles (see Exodus 23:16), which celebrated God's presence among His people and symbolized the end-time harvest of souls that have been saved.

Pentecost, the second of the annual feasts, was also known as the Feast of Firstfruits. In addition to celebrating the beginning of the harvest, the Feast of Pentecost also foreshadowed the coming of the Holy Spirit for the first time. Pentecost occurred 50 days after Passover. Just as Jesus Christ, the "Lamb of God who takes away the sin of the world" (Jn. 1:29b), died on Passover, the Holy Spirit came 50 days later during Pentecost, signifying the beginning of the great spiritual harvest of souls.

Every person is required to "appear" before God three times: in salvation, in the baptism in the Holy Spirit, and in the final ingathering of souls, thus fulfilling the purpose and meaning of the three feasts: Passover, Pentecost, Tabernacles.

Three times in his letters, Paul refers to the Holy Spirit as the "guarantee" or "down payment" of our full spiritual inheritance, which shall be bestowed on us when we get to Heaven. Being filled with the Holy Spirit is the manifestation of our citizenship in God's Kingdom. In the same way that one nation has ambassadors and embassies in foreign countries, the baptism in the Holy Spirit identifies us as citizens of Heaven while we are on earth. Speaking in tongues is the "native" tongue, the native "language" of Heaven. Every citizen of Heaven should both speak and understand the "native" language of tongues! Paul wrote to the Corinthians, "Though I speak with the tongues of men and of angels, but have not love, I have become sounding brass or a clanging cymbal" (1 Cor. 13:1).

Speaking in Tongues: the Voice of the Lord

Speaking in tongues is the first and primary biblical manifestation of being baptized in the Holy Spirit:

And suddenly there came a sound from heaven, as of a rushing mighty wind, and it filled the whole house where they were sitting. Then there appeared to them divided tongues, as of fire, and one sat upon each of them. And they were all filled with the Holy Spirit and began to speak with other tongues, as the Spirit gave them utterance (Acts 2:2-4).

It is "the voice of the Lord" in the same way that inspired prophetic utterance is.

Psalm 29 is a song about the voice of the Lord that I believe also describes the aspects and effects of speaking in tongues.

Give unto the Lord, O you mighty ones, give unto the Lord glory and strength. Give unto the Lord the glory due to His name; worship the Lord in the beauty of holiness. The voice of the Lord is over the waters; the God of glory thunders; the Lord is over many waters. The voice of the Lord is powerful: the voice of the Lord is full of majesty. The voice of the Lord breaks the cedars, yes, the Lord splinters the cedars of Lebanon. He makes them also skip like a calf, Lebanon and Sirion like a young wild ox. The voice of the Lord divides the flames of fire. The voice of the Lord shakes the wilderness; the Lord shakes the Wilderness of Kadesh. The voice of the Lord makes the deer give birth, and strips the forests bare; and in His temple everyone says, "Glory!" The Lord sat enthroned at the Flood, and the Lord sits as King forever. The Lord will give strength to His people; the Lord will bless His people with peace (Psalm 29:1-11).

This psalm begins with a command for us to do two things: give the Lord the glory due His name, and worship the Lord in the beauty of holiness. Both of these we can obey wonderfully through tongues. As we speak in tongues, pray in tongues, and sing in tongues, we give God the glory due His name. Tongues enables us to praise and glorify God. When we pray in tongues we worship in the particular beauty of the Holy Spirit. Just as Abraham's servant in Genesis 24 was sent to find a bride for Isaac, the Holy Spirit was sent to identify, prepare, adorn, and beautify the Bride chosen for God's only Son.

Psalm 29:3-4 provides an apt description of speaking in tongues: "The voice of the Lord is over the waters; the God of glory thunders; the Lord is over many waters. The voice of the Lord is powerful: the voice of the Lord is full of majesty." Revelation 1:15 describes the voice of Jesus, our resurrected

Savior and our Bridegroom, as "the sound of many waters." Jesus plainly states in John 7:37-38 that for anyone who believes on Him, out of his heart (not mind) rivers of living water would flow. In the very next verse John makes it clear that Jesus was referring to the Holy Spirit.

The manifestation of the Holy Spirit is similar to rivers of water. Jesus said that we would receive power when the Holy Spirit came upon us (see Acts 1:8). When the "water" of the Holy Spirit comes down, God's voice will be heard. This happened first on the day of Pentecost, where God's voice was manifested in the believers through speaking in tongues: "They...began to speak with other tongues, as the Spirit gave them utterance" (Acts 2:4). Speaking in tongues is the manifestation of the living river of the Holy Sprit coming out of the believer's spirit and it is powerful!

Verses 5-7 of Psalm 29 describe the power of speaking in tongues: "The voice of the Lord breaks the cedars, yes the Lord splinters the cedars of Lebanon. He makes them also skip like a calf, Lebanon and Sirion like a young wild ox. The voice of the Lord divides the flames of fire." On the day of Pentecost, the Holy Spirit manifested Himself in "divided tongues of fire" (Acts 2:3). According to the psalmist, the power of speaking or praying in tongues can splinter strong cedars. Trees in Scripture often represent rulers, spiritual or natural. Speaking in tongues breaks the power of even the strongest natural leaders and sends principalities and powers fleeing!

"The voice of the Lord shakes the wilderness; the Lord shakes the Wilderness of Kadesh" (Ps. 29:8). Kadesh is the Valley of Eshcol where Joshua and his men went to spy out the land that God had promised to give them. In the wilderness of Kadesh the spies cut down a branch with one cluster of grapes so large that it required two men to carry it back! In Hebrew, the word for "shakes" is hil, the same descriptive word used of David's dance as he returned the ark of the Covenant to Jerusalem (see 2 Sam. 6): an ecstatic twirling, like a whirlwind in power, turning round and round. Such is the nature and power, but also the spiritual worship, of speaking in tongues. Just as David was so caught up in worship that he cared nothing about his personal appearance or reputation, as we pray in the Spirit, no matter what our circumstances, we are carried into a place of spiritual worship that ushers in the victory of God manifest in the presence of Jesus.

What difficulties are you facing today? What opposition are you encountering in life? Why don't you start praying in the Spirit right now, enter the realm that King David entered, and start getting the victory?

Speaking in tongues brings forth the fruit of our spiritual promises in God. There will always be those who despise the Holy Spirit. King David's own wife did! Michal called her husband's ecstatic spiritual worship a thing of the flesh—unbecoming foolishness for a king! Her carnal opinion did not affect David in the least. Instead, he told her, in effect, "If you didn't like that, brace yourself because I am only going to get more radical" (see 2 Sam. 6:14-16). Every Christian must choose between obedience to the Holy Spirit or respectability before men.

The Voice of the Lord in Personal Crisis

Psalm 29:9a exclaims, "The voice of the Lord makes the deer give birth, and strips the forests bare." My wife, Bonnie, had an extraordinary experience of hearing the voice of the Lord during her fourth pregnancy with our son Aaron. Here is the account in her own words:

> In 1985 I was pregnant with our fourth child. Early in the pregnancy, I started hemorrhaging, and learned that I had "placenta previa centralis," a very severe illness of the placenta where it does not attach to the uterus correctly. Our doctor said, "Okay, you just need to go to bed," and things went

from bad to worse. By the time I was 25 weeks pregnant, my water broke and I was in and out of labor all the time, continuing to hemorrhage. At that point the doctor recommended that we have a "D & C." We did not take their advice because, in our spirits, we heard the Lord say, "Wait." So we waited. It was a mess, a really terrible mess.

Finally, they were going to take the baby, so I went into the hospital under the care of my doctor. He was a wonderful man, a Sikh, and had delivered all three of our previous children. He had been watching our family for a long time, and we knew that it was time for him to see the reality of our faith, how real Jesus was to us, and all the amazing ways in which He had blessed us.

As they rushed me into surgery for a C-section, the operating room was filled with people. Fourteen people from the neo-natal intensive care unit were on hand to deal with the baby, if it was born alive, and a separate group of people was there to take care of me. I remember that as the anesthesiologist approached me, it appeared in my mind's eye like a cartoon: a guy with a big needle and a little hat on his head coming toward me to put me to sleep.

At the same time, another man entered the operating room. It was Jesus. His physical form was more like a cloud, but there was a definite silhouette. Even as the anesthesiologist approached, Jesus walked right to the head of the stretcher where I was lying. It was funny because, even though He was behind me, I could still see Him. That is one of the wonderful things about the Lord; He is everywhere, and we will experience God just as though He is right in front of us. As He came in, something came out of

Him, something that I call the "voice of God." It was not a human voice. He did not speak English words. His voice was a powerful force, like water, electricity, lightning, flood, fire, love, creation, all in one—just an indescribable power. His voice was like a sound, but also more than a sound, more than words.

As He spoke, His voice came down my body, and as it hit me, my mouth opened. I pointed at the surgeon, and, without hesitation or thinking it through first, said to him, "I can have this baby naturally." The doctor looked back at me in amazement. That voice traveled down my body and surrounded whatever was in my womb. Suddenly, there was a soft "pop," followed by five little "mews" like a baby kitten. When I heard this, I pointed at the doctor and his face turned ashen. He was holding this mass of something in his hands. His eyes were bulging and the whole room went into a flurry. I blurted out, "It's a boy, isn't it?" He nodded.

This was beyond impossible, and yet Aaron was born. He was all bruised up. At birth his thigh was the size of my wedding ring. My wedding ring could fit on his little thigh. Aaron's birth weight was one pound and 3 ounces, but he immediately lost his birth water weight, so his weight dropped to less than one pound. We have pictures of Aaron lying next to a toothbrush, where he and the toothbrush are the same length. He had a staph infection, and blood in his spinal column. His little ears had not even curled up; they were flat flaps of skin on the side of his face. Everything seemed such a disaster that it was hard even to think about it. Here was our newborn son, and every prognosis was that he was going to die.

The voice of the Lord brought about the supernatural birth of our son, who had only been in the womb for five months. Today, Aaron is seventeen years old, healthy, strong, and intelligent. He loves the Lord, does well in school, and is active in his church youth group. All throughout her pregnancy, Bonnie lay in bed for three months and magnified God in her prayer language. Now every time we look at Aaron we know God is real and His mercy is everlasting. We recall how the voice of the Lord came mightily to Bonnie, delivered Aaron, and then completely healed and restored him. Speaking in tongues is one of the weapons of our spiritual warfare, mighty in God for pulling down strongholds and making us triumphant in all circumstances.

Speaking in Tongues: the Bridal Language of Intimacy

"The Lord sat enthroned at the Flood, and the Lord sits as King forever" (Ps. 29:10). This verse refers not to the flood of Noah, but to Moses' parting of the Red Sea with the rod of authority. Isaiah 59:19b says, "When the enemy comes in like a flood, the Spirit of the Lord will lift up a standard against him." Just as when Moses raised his rod at the Red Sea, and God delivered His people from the army of Pharaoh that was chasing them, so today when the enemy chases the people of God, the Spirit of the Lord will raise a standard against him. For me, this chapter indicates that speaking in tongues enthrones God as King and parts the greatest barrier so we can walk in freedom just as Israel walked through the Red Sea and watched it close over Pharaoh's warriors and chariots.

The final verse of Psalm 29 promises strength and peace: "The Lord will give strength to His people; The Lord will bless His people with peace" (Ps. 29:11). As His people pray in the Spirit, the Lord gives to them His wholeness and well being. Jude 1:20 encourages us to "[build] yourselves up on your most holy faith, praying in the Spirit." God created tongues as the supernatural language of Heaven and gave it to us through the baptism in the Holy Spirit that we might have the words and understanding by the Spirit to pray effectively when we do not know how or what to pray with our natural minds.

The "voice of many waters," the voice of Jesus, is the voice of the Bridegroom. Speaking in tongues is the believer's bridal language of intimacy with the Bridegroom. In the same manner that a man and wife commune with one another in physical intimacy, through speaking in tongues we commune in spiritual intimacy with Christ our Bridegroom. Speaking or praying to Him in tongues gives expression of our spiritual love for Jesus, love given by the Holy Spirit. Speaking in tongues is an expression of our union, our covenant with Christ. The Holy Spirit enables the Bride of Christ to communicate with Him in His native language, the language not of earth, but of Heaven, the language not of the carnal mind or earthly intellect, but the language of the Spirit, of the heart of God.

John wrote the final revelation of Jesus Christ as he was "in the Spirit," seeing, experiencing, understanding, and recording spiritual truth. In Rev. 22:16 John hears the Bridegroom speak and declare Himself: "I am the Root and the Offspring of David, Bright and Morning Star." In other words, He is about to appear. In response to this revelation, John hears the Spirit and the Bride—the Church on earth—say "Come!" Praying in the Spirit ushers in the appearing of the Lord. In addition, John said, "Let him who hears say 'come.' And let him who thirsts come. Whoever desires, let him take the water of life freely" (Rev. 22:17b). Speaking in tongues draws the thirsty to Christ and prays in the harvest. Whoever comes to Christ receives the river of the Holy Spirit freely, without measure, without restriction, and without any rebuke.

The apostle Paul said that while he spoke in simple words of earthly language so that an unbeliever might hear and receive the gospel, he thanked God that he spoke in tongues more than all to whom he wrote! (see 1 Cor. 14:18) Paul understood the value of being able to speak the language of God.

Eugene Peterson's contemporary paraphrase of Scripture called The Message exquisitely captures the power and force of Psalm 29:

> *Bravo, God, bravo! Gods and all angels shout, "Encore!" In awe before the glory, in awe before God's visible power. Stand at attention! Dress your best to honor Him! God thunders across the waters, brilliant, His voice and His face, streaming brightness— God, across the flood waters. God's thunder tympanic, God's thunder symphonic. God's thunder smashes cedars, God topples the northern cedars. The mountain ranges skip like spring colts, The high ridges jump like wild kid goats. God's thunder spits fire. God thunders, the wilderness quakes; He makes the desert of Kadesh shake. God's thunder sets the oak trees dancing a wild dance, whirling; the pelting rain strips their branches. We fall to our knees—we call out, "Glory!" Above the floodwaters is God's throne from which His power flows, from which He rules the world. God makes His people strong. God gives His people peace* (Psalm 29:1-11 The Message).

Because Paul understood the language of God and its importance, he was one of the most effective people who ever lived. When he met Christ he was changed forever. The Holy Spirit transformed Paul's life from the inside out. The secret of Paul's success and effectiveness was, among other things, his understanding of the place and power in his life of the language of the Spirit.

Chapter Seven

THE SECRET OF PAUL'S EFFECTIVENESS

Next to the Lord Jesus Christ Himself, probably no one has had a greater influence on the life, growth, and history of the Christian church than has the apostle Paul. Aside from being one of the most highly educated and brilliantly intellectual men of his day, this Jew from the city of Tarsus was also a man of great passion. Paul never did anything half-heartedly. Whether as a zealous Pharisee persecuting the followers of Jesus, or later as a persecuted but faithful and tireless follower of that same Jesus, Paul committed himself heart and soul. There was no other way for him. Someone once said that Paul did not become a fanatic when he came to Christ. Paul was always a fanatic; he merely switched sides.

Here is a man who, under the inspiration of the Holy Spirit, wrote half the books of the New Testament, accounting for over one-fourth of its total volume, more than any other individual. Paul established, nurtured, taught, and encouraged churches throughout the Roman Empire and, according to tradition, even carried the gospel as far as Gaul and Spain. He is credited with developing or at least articulating most of the theology of the early Church. Over the course of his life Paul endured hardship and travail that would have killed many other men. Most significant, perhaps, was the undeniably supernatural nature of Paul's ministry. Everywhere he went, Paul's ministry manifested the power of the Holy Spirit. "Now God worked unusual miracles by the hands of Paul, so that even handkerchiefs or aprons were brought from his body to the sick, and the diseases left them and the evil spirits went out of them" (Acts 19:11-12). In my opinion, Paul's was the greatest New Testament ministry after that of Christ Himself.

How did he do it? What set Paul apart to make him so singularly influential and effective? What was the hidden key to the power and anointing that flowed in his life? I believe the answer can be found in two statements that Paul himself made in his first letter to the Christian believers in Corinth. These statements define Paul's "philosophy of ministry," so to speak—the "cornerstones" of everything he did. They are closely related, the first statement being the key to the second.

Early in his letter Paul makes this declaration: "For I determined not to know anything among you except Jesus Christ and Him crucified" (1 Cor. 2:2). Here in a nutshell is Paul's purpose, his entire reason for living. The second statement occurs much later, toward the end of the letter. Because it sounds at first like a simple passing comment, the significance of this second statement has been generally overlooked by many. Paul says simply,

"I thank my God I speak with tongues more than you all" (1 Cor. 14:18).

I believe there is more here than meets the eye. With these simple words Paul reveals a major secret of the power and vitality of his "inner man"—his personal spiritual life—and his relationship with the Lord.

In the life of Paul we see an example of true discipleship. Paul lived all out for Jesus. He knew great joy as well as deep pain and sorrow. In many ways his life as an apostle was a lonely one. Several of his letters contain poignant passages where he expresses his deep appreciation for those—sometimes few—who love and support him, and shares the ache in his heart for the ones who have abandoned him or rejected his message. There is evidence that many first-century churches in Asia Minor (today's Turkey)—churches that Paul worked particularly hard for and were especially dear to him—ultimately rejected his apostleship. Nevertheless, Paul found an unquenchable fountain of strength and hope in the presence of the Holy Spirit, through whom he was connected to the glory of Heaven.

Years ago, novelist Taylor Caldwell wrote a fictionalized chronicle of the life of this fearless and untiring apostle. The title of her novel, *Great Lion of God*, says it all. Paul was indeed one of the great "lions" of God: strong, tenacious, and fierce and unyielding when confronting the enemies of his Lord and of his beloved churches.

A man of amazing gifts, Paul received stunning and profound revelations that have shaped and enriched the Body of Christ even up to today. Thanks to Paul we can more fully comprehend the meaning of the cross. Because of Paul we can better understand redemption and sanctification, salvation by grace through faith, and the freedom we have in Christ. It was Paul who penned the greatest treatise on love ever written. It was Paul who gave us such memorable phrases as "to live is Christ and to die is gain," "I have been crucified with Christ," "Christ in you, the hope of glory," and "I have fought the good fight, I have finished the race, I have kept the faith." The range and richness of Paul's revelations are truly magnificent. Apart from Jesus Himself, no one else can compare. Probably the only one who comes close is Moses, who spent 80 days in the direct presence of God, who revealed the Law to him.

In the end, the secret of Paul's success is very simple. The effectiveness of his life is due to his commitment to those two fundamental principles: "For I determined not to know anything among you except Jesus Christ and Him crucified," and "I thank my God I speak with tongues more than you all."

Jesus Christ and Him Crucified

B efore he came to Christ, Paul, like most other Pharisees, took great pride in his learning and in his thorough knowledge of the Scriptures. Pharisees were the top religious leaders among the Jews, experts in the Law and in all the traditions of the elders. They zealously exceeded all other Jews in their meticulous observance of every "jot and tittle" of every commandment. Consequently, they believed themselves to be more acceptable to God than anyone else. In their minds, righteousness meant strict outward observance of the law. They had no concept of a heart transformation in the inner man.

All of this changed for Paul when he found Christ. Paul discovered that without Jesus, none of his great learning mattered for anything, because it could not make him righteous before God. This insight led him later to write of his fellow Israelites, and especially his Pharisee colleagues:

> *Brethren, my heart's desire and prayer to God for Israel is that they may be saved. For I bear them witness that they have a zeal for God, but not according to knowledge. For they being ignorant of God's righteousness, and seeking to establish their own righteousness, have not submitted to the righteousness of God. For Christ is the end of the law for righteousness to everyone who believes* (Romans 10:1-4).

Enlightened by the Spirit of God, Paul came to understand that the Law was not an end in itself but pointed to

Christ, who was the "righteousness of God," and the fulfillment of everything the Law anticipated. In fulfilling the Law, Christ became "the end of the law." The Lord Jesus replaced the Law as the central focus in Paul's life. All his life Paul had believed that the Law was the foundation of righteousness. Now he learned that Christ was the foundation of the Law. The purpose of the Law was to point people to Jesus. Only in Christ could true righteousness be found. He alone is the true foundation for our faith. Paul explained it to the Corinthians this way:

> *According to the grace of God which was given to me, as a wise master builder I have laid the foundation, and another builds on it. But let each one take heed how he builds on it. For no other foundation can anyone lay than that which is laid, which is Jesus Christ* (1 Corinthians 3:10-11).

It was this transformation of heart and mind that led Paul to lay aside the complexity of the Law for the simplicity of the cross and the wisdom of man for the power of God.

> *And I, brethren, when I came to you, did not come with excellence of speech or of wisdom declaring to you the testimony of God. For I determined not to know anything among you except Jesus Christ and Him crucified. I was with you in weakness, in fear, and in much trembling. And my speech and my preaching were not with persuasive words of human wisdom, but in demonstration of the Spirit and of power, that your faith should not be in the wisdom of men but in the power of God* (1 Corinthians 2:1-5).

The principal key to the spiritual power in Paul's life and work was his singular focus on Jesus Christ. Paul made a great impact on his world because he depended not on his own wisdom or abilities but on the power of God through the Holy Spirit. That is where the secret lies. Christ is the source of the power. He is the one who gives the Holy Spirit, from whom the anointing comes. There is no other foundation, no other message than "Jesus Christ and Him crucified."

This truth was fundamental for Paul. Paul was *sold out* to Jesus Christ. His life belonged no longer to him but to Christ, whose blood had purchased him and delivered him from death and condemnation. Paul lived solely for the service and glory of his Lord. His letters are full of references to his surrendered life:

For to me, to live is Christ, and to die is gain (Philippians 1:21).

From now on let no one trouble me, for I bear in my body the marks of the Lord Jesus (Galatians 6:17).

I have been crucified with Christ; it is no longer I who live, but Christ lives in me; and the life which I now live in the flesh I live by faith in the Son of God, who loved me and gave Himself for me (Galatians 2:20).

I have fought the good fight, I have finished the race, I have kept the faith (2 Timothy 4:7).

As far as Paul was concerned, nothing was more important or valuable than knowing Jesus. His heritage, his education, his credentials as a Pharisee, his racial purity as a Jew—all of these were meaningless without Christ. Compared to Christ, nothing else mattered.

But what things were gain to me, these I have counted loss for Christ. Yet indeed I also count all things loss for the excellence of the knowledge of Christ Jesus my Lord, for whom I have suffered the loss of all things, and count them as rubbish, that I may gain Christ and be found in Him, not having my own righteousness, which is from the law, but that which is through faith in Christ, the righteousness which is from God by faith; that I may know Him and the power of His resurrection, and the fellowship of His sufferings, being conformed to His death, if, by any means, I may attain to the resurrection from the dead. Not that I have already attained, or am already perfected; but I press on, that I may lay hold of that for which Christ Jesus has also laid hold of me. Brethren, I do not count myself to have apprehended; but one thing I do, forgetting those things which are behind and reaching forward to those things which are ahead, I press toward the goal for the prize of the upward call of God in Christ Jesus (Philippians 3:7-14).

The Deep Things of God

Paul realized that human wisdom by itself would never lead to spiritual wisdom or knowledge of the deep things of God. Only the Holy Spirit could impart that wisdom. This is one reason why Paul placed such a premium of value on knowing Christ and being submissive to His Spirit. Through divine revelation Paul understood that there was a whole realm of reality, wisdom, and truth that was unknown to and unknowable by human wisdom. He refers to it as a mystery.

However, we speak wisdom among those who are mature, yet not the wisdom of this age, nor of the rulers of this age, who are coming to nothing. But we speak the wisdom of God in a mystery, the hidden wisdom which God ordained before the ages for our glory, which none of the rulers of this age knew; for had they known, they would not have crucified the Lord of glory. But as it is written: "Eye has not seen, nor ear heard, nor have entered into the heart of man the things which God has prepared for those who love Him." But God has revealed them to us through His Spirit. For the Spirit searches all things, yes, the deep things of God. For what man knows the things of a man except the spirit of the man which is in him? Even so no one knows the things of God except the Spirit of God. Now we have received, not the spirit of the world, but the Spirit who is from God, that we might know the things that have been freely given to us by God. (1 Corinthians 2:6-12).

Paul is telling us how to come into the glory. He had touched it himself. He had connected with the glory of the Lord and had seen Jesus face-to-face. Now he is revealing the secret: We connect with the glory through the Holy Spirit. That is the only way. The cross of Jesus makes our connection with the glory possible; the Holy Spirit gives us access. Verse 10 makes it clear that the deep things of God are knowable to us only by the revelation of God, and the agent of that revelation is the Holy Spirit.

If we want revelation and divine insight, we must have the Holy Spirit in us and depend on Him daily. The Holy Spirit "searches all things," and especially the "deep things of God." He knows the heart of God. He knows the mind and thoughts of God. He knows the will of God. These things are unknowable by the mind or spirit of man. God wants us to know them, however. He has freely given them to us, and the Holy Spirit is the One who makes them known to us. If we desire to connect with the deep things of God, we must connect with the Holy Spirit. Speaking in tongues is a vital tool for making that connection.

As believers we have a direct connection to God, our Father, because the Holy Spirit, who is our Advocate and Helper, and Jesus Christ, who is our High Priest, both make constant intercession on our behalf.

*Likewise the Spirit also helps in our weaknesses. For
we do not know what we should pray for as we ought,
but the Spirit Himself makes intercession for us with
groanings which cannot be uttered. Now He who
searches the hearts knows what the mind of the Spirit is, because He makes intercession for the saints
according to the will of God* (Romans 8:26-27).

*Who is he who condemns? It is Christ who died, and
furthermore is also risen, who is even at the right
hand of God, who also makes intercession for us*
(Romans 8:34).

*Therefore He [Jesus] is also able to save to the
uttermost those who come to God through Him,
since He always lives to make intercession for them*
(Hebrews 7:25).

The reason Paul accomplished so much for the KIngdom
of God is because he kept his eyes fixed on Jesus and main-
tained an intimate personal relationship with the Holy Spirit.
He was connected to the glory and thereby walked in wisdom,
insight, revelation, and power. The more he drank of the Spirit, the thirstier he became; the more he learned of the deep
things of God, the more he wanted to learn. I believe this is
why Paul placed such personal value on the gift of tongues.
Speaking in tongues was like a lubricant that greatly enhanced
Paul's ability to communicate with and receive from his Lord.

I Speak With Tongues More Than You All

Paul's personal statement regarding tongues occurs within
a much broader discussion of tongues, prophecy, and
order in public worship. It is important to establish some context in order to understand where Paul is coming from.

The church in Corinth was having problems with its public worship. Apparently, there was a lot of disorder in the assembly, including disagreement and even competition over the value and "prestige" of some spiritual gifts over others. People who possessed certain supposedly "higher" gifts looked down on others who did not. Confusion and division ruled the day.

Paul addresses these problems in chapter 14 of First Corinthians. Right on the heels of the great "love chapter" which extols agape—the divine love—as the greatest gift of all, Paul writes:

> *Pursue love, and desire spiritual gifts, but especially that you may prophesy. For he who speaks in a tongue does not speak to men but to God, for no one understands him; however, in the spirit he speaks mysteries. But he who prophesies speaks edification and exhortation and comfort to men. He who speaks in a tongue edifies himself, but he who prophesies edifies the church. I wish you all spoke with tongues, but even more that you prophesied; for he who prophesies is greater than he who speaks with tongues, unless indeed he interprets, that the church may receive edification* (1 Corinthians 14:1-5).

In the verses that follow, Paul stresses the importance of speaking words in the meeting place that are understandable by everyone over words spoken in an unknown tongue that no one will understand unless someone is present to interpret. Then he says,

> *I thank my God I speak with tongues more than you all; yet in the church I would rather speak five words with my understanding, that I may teach others also, than ten thousand words in a tongue* (1 Corinthians 14:18-19).

Many people who try to downplay the significance or validity of speaking in tongues for today point to this passage in support of their position because Paul clearly gives precedence to prophecy over tongues. It is important to note, however, that Paul's instructions are in the context of *public worship*, not private prayer. Indeed, in public worship prophesying is more important than tongues because it can be understood by everyone and therefore can edify or build up everyone. If unbelievers are present, they may be brought to repentance and faith. Speaking in tongues is valuable in public worship when interpretation is available, because the interpretation can then edify everyone present.

The principal value and power of speaking in tongues lie in the edification that comes to the individual in his or her personal prayer and devotional life and communion with the Lord. Viewed from this perspective, it is clear that Paul valued the gift of tongues very highly. Consider these statements:

> *For he who speaks in a tongue does not speak to men but to God, for no one understands him; however, in the spirit he speaks mysteries* (1 Corinthians 14:2).

> *He who speaks in a tongue edifies himself...*(1 Corinthians 14:4a).

> *I wish you all spoke with tongues...*(1 Corinthians 14:5a).

> *For if I pray in a tongue, my spirit prays...*(1 Corinthians 14:14a).

> *I thank my God I speak with tongues more than you all* (1 Corinthians 14:18).

> *If anyone speaks in a tongue, let there be two or at the most three, each in turn, and let one interpret. But if there is no interpreter, let him keep silent in*

church, and let him speak to himself and to God
(1 Corinthians 14:27-28).

*Therefore, brethren, desire earnestly to prophesy,
and do not forbid to speak with tongues* (1 Corinthians 14:39).

These words are part of the accepted canon of holy Scripture; part of the divinely inspired Word of God. Paul's statement, "I thank my God I speak in tongues more than you all," was preserved as part of the New Testament, thereby receiving God's "stamp of approval" as true and accurate. In those words lie the greatest key, aside from "Jesus Christ and Him crucified," to connecting with the glory of God.

Speaking in tongues is a devotional language. It is not something that we can develop in five minutes a day. We may start there, but we should grow far beyond that level. The Holy Spirit has given us a wonderful gift that invites us to reach out and touch the glory of God. Paul took the challenge. He became an expert in speaking in tongues and of praying and walking in the Spirit.

The key was hunger. Paul was insatiably hungry for Jesus. He thirsted constantly for the fellowship of the Holy Spirit. What was the result? Look at the evidence of his life. Even today, nearly 2,000 years later, the world and especially the Church, still feels the effects and reaps the benefits of the life of this great lion of God.

For us, too, hunger is the key. Do you want to connect with the glory of God, with His revelation, and with the awesome signs and wonders He wants to pour out on these end-time generations? How hungry are you? Are you hungry for Jesus? Are you hungry for the Spirit? Are you hungry for the deep things of God? Are you hungry for the glory?

Chapter Eight

HUNGRY FOR THE GLORY

Through the years I have heard many people ask questions like, "Should all Christians speak in tongues?" "Is the baptism of the Holy Spirit really necessary?" "Can't we get along just fine as believers without all that stuff?" "Is speaking in tongues the only way for us to 'connect' with the Holy Spirit?"

At the heart of these questions lies the old debate over the present role and ministry of the Holy Spirit in the church. Many believers contend that being baptized in the Spirit is not "necessary" for a Christian, and claim that they can live satisfying and effective Christian lives without speaking in tongues. For me, however, this begs the question, "Why settle for less than the best?" If the baptism of the Holy Spirit, along with speaking in tongues and all its other advantages, is readily available to all believers, why would we not want to avail ourselves of everything it has to offer?

Satisfaction is a relative quality. What satisfies you may not satisfy me, and what satisfies me may not satisfy someone else. The degree to which we experience the presence and power of the Holy Spirit in our lives basically depends on three things: our level of expectancy, our willingness, and our hunger.

In the early years of the twentieth century, a young man emigrated from Europe to the United States. Being of limited means, he had scraped and saved for quite some time in order to have the money for his steamship ticket. Finally, with ticket in hand, he packed his few belongings, including enough bread and cheese to sustain him over the weeklong voyage.

During the journey he passed his days peacefully by walking the decks or resting in his cabin. Every now and then he would pass by the ship's dining hall and savor the aromas of the rich and varied dishes served there. Sometimes he even stood and watched through the window as other passengers enjoyed their meals. Then, knowing he could never afford such a banquet, he would hurry to his cabin and parcel out some of his bread and cheese.

On the final day of the trip, the young man stood on deck in the shadow of the Statue of Liberty, nibbling on the last of his bread and cheese as the ship approached New York Harbor. The ship's purser passed by and, seeing the young man by the railing, asked, "Have you enjoyed your trip, sir?"

"Yes, very much."

"I notice that you are eating some old bread and cheese. Were the meals on board not to your liking?"

"I don't understand."

Did you find the dining room food objectionable?"

"Oh, no. I've been eating this bread and cheese all week because I couldn't afford to eat in the dining room. I had only enough money to buy my ticket."

With a surprised look on his face, the purser said, "I am so sorry, sir! Didn't you realize that the price of your ticket paid for everything, not only your berth but all your meals as well?"

This young immigrant had all the resources of the ship available to him but he did not know it. He felt he had to content himself with the meager food he had brought with him. His bread and cheese nourished him during the trip, but he could have enjoyed so much more.

I believe it is the same way with the things of the Spirit. As long as we are satisfied with just bread and cheese we will have little motivation to seek anything more, even though the Holy Spirit has laid out an abundant feast for us. We will never pursue that which we do not desire. How can we slake a thirst or satisfy a hunger we don't know we have? Maybe we feel somehow that the feast is for others but not for us, or we may even have trouble believing there *is* a feast.

Our expectations in the realm of the Spirit will be determined largely by the teachings we have received and by what we believe about Him. These things in turn determine our hunger. Like the young European immigrant, many Christians do not realize that their "ticket" (salvation through Jesus Christ) paid for everything, and that all the boundless resources of the Spirit of God are available to them. So, in the presence of a feast, they content themselves with bread and cheese. I say, if we are going to make the passage anyway, why not enjoy the trip to the fullest?

Show Me Your Glory

Paul the apostle was a hungry man. We saw in the last chapter how his intense hunger for Jesus and the things of the Spirit lay behind his great success and effectiveness in ministry. All the great men and women of God throughout history, whether in the Bible or in later years, have always been hungry people. Their hearts crave the bread of life and their spirits thirst for God's presence. The opening verses of Psalm 42 express this well: "As the deer pants for the water brooks, so pants my soul for You, O God. My soul thirsts for God, for the living God. When shall I come and appear before God?" (Ps. 42:1-2).

It is the hungry whom the Lord satisfies. That is why Jesus said, "Blessed are those who hunger and thirst for righteousness, for they shall be filled" (Mt. 5:6), and "Ask, and it will be given to you; seek, and you will find; knock, and it will be opened to you. For everyone who asks receives, and he who seeks finds, and to him who knocks it will be opened" (Mt. 7:7-8).

Moses, too, was a hungry man. Once he got a taste of God's presence, he could not get enough. Even the singular opportunity of spending 80 days alone with God on Mt. Sinai did not satisfy his hunger, because a day came not long after where Moses boldly asked God, "Show me Your glory."

> *Then Moses said to the Lord, "See, You say to me, 'Bring up this people.' But You have not let me know whom You will send with me. Yet You have said, 'I know you by name, and you have also found grace in My sight.' Now therefore, I pray, if I have found grace in Your sight, show me now Your way, that I may know You and that I may find grace in Your sight. And consider that this nation is Your people." And He said, "My Presence will go with you, and I will give you rest." Then he said to Him, "If Your Presence does not go with us, do not bring us up from here. For how then will it be known that Your*

people and I have found grace in Your sight, except You go with us? So we shall be separate, Your people and I, from all the people who are upon the face of the earth." So the Lord said to Moses, "I will also do this thing that you have spoken; for you have found grace in My sight, and I know you by name." And he said, "Please, show me Your glory" (Exodus 33:12-18).

God had said to Moses, "I know you by name and you have also found grace in My sight." As great as that was, Moses wanted more: "Please, show me Your glory." God had promised Moses, "My Presence will go with you, and I will give you rest." It was an awesome promise, but Moses wanted more: "Please, show me Your glory." Moses was a man who entered the cloud of God's presence, and of whom it was said that God spoke to him "face to face, as a man speaks to his friend" (Ex. 33:11a). A wonderful tribute, but Moses wanted more.

Moses was hungry for the glory of God. He wanted to know God and find grace in His sight. He recognized also that knowing God was not accomplished in an afternoon, but was a progressive relationship growing out of much time spent in God's presence. Moses' words in verse 13 reflect this. The Amplified Version brings out the sense of the Hebrew better:

Now therefore, I pray You, if I have found favor in Your sight, show me now Your way, that I may know You [progressively become more deeply and intimately acquainted with You, perceiving and recognizing and understanding more strongly and clearly] and that I may find favor in Your sight. And [Lord, do] consider that this nation is Your people (Exodus 33:13 AMP).

Like Moses, we need to realize that we have not "arrived" simply because we are Christians or even because we have been baptized in the Holy Spirit and speak in tongues. It is easy to get satisfied and lazy, wanting to rest on our laurels and be content with where we are spiritually. Moses was never satisfied; he was always seeking to get closer to God. Knowing the Lord is a progressive walk. How far we travel depends on how hungry we are for the glory of the Lord. Hunger motivates us; desperate hunger will drive us to do whatever we have to do to be satisfied.

A Passion for Jesus

Very little of worth in life is accomplished without passion. Many of the greatest achievements and milestones in science, medicine, social reform, judicial reform, and other human disciplines were born out of desperate need or someone's passionate commitment to a cause. The abolition of slavery throughout the British Empire in the early nineteenth century was due in large part to the untiring, patient, and passionate work of one man, William Wilberforce, a member of Parliament who was also a committed follower of Christ. Thanks to Dr. Jonas Salk, whose passionate pursuit of a weapon against polio led to an effective vaccine in 1950, one of the most feared diseases of modern times was virtually eradicated.

Passion is important in the spiritual realm as well. If we are to grow in the grace and knowledge of the Lord and be effective ministers of His love, compassion, and power, we must be passionate about Jesus, about His presence, and about the outworking of His destiny for each of us. We need to be bold enough to approach God's throne of grace and say, "I'm hungry for more of you, Lord. Fill me with Your Spirit. Let Your glory shine through me."

The baptism of the Holy Spirit, with its accompanying sign of speaking in tongues, is important to us for several reasons. First, it connects us to the glory of God, and works to conform us to the image of Christ. "Now the Lord is the Spirit; and where the Spirit of the Lord is, there is liberty. But we all, with unveiled face, beholding as in a mirror the glory of the Lord, are being transformed into the same image from glory to glory, just as by the Spirit of the Lord" (2 Cor. 3:17-18). The words "unveiled face" refer to Moses, who found it necessary, after being in God's presence, to veil his face because it literally glowed from the experience. Through the presence of the Holy Spirit, however, we can see the glory of the Lord "as in a mirror," and the Spirit is transforming us into His likeness.

Second, the language of the Spirit helps us grow in our faith. "But you, beloved, building yourselves up on your most holy faith, praying in the Holy Spirit, keep yourselves in the love of God, looking for the mercy of our Lord Jesus Christ unto eternal life" (Jude 1:20-21). Praying in the Spirit brings us in tune with the heart and mind of God and helps us walk in the will of Christ. Through the ministry of the Holy Spirit we come into intimate knowledge of Jesus, who is Truth.

> *However, when He, the Spirit of truth, has come, He will guide you into all truth; for He will not speak on His own authority, but whatever He hears He will speak; and He will tell you things to come. He will glorify Me, for He will take of what is Mine and declare it to you. All things that the Father has are Mine. Therefore I said that He will take of Mine and declare it to you"* (John 16:13-15).

A third value of the language of the Spirit is that it helps place a spiritual covering and protection over ourselves and our families. Just as there are pestilences in the natural world, there are also pestilences in the realm of the spirit. It is the anointing and the blood of Jesus that protect us, and the Holy Spirit is the vehicle by whom they come to us.

Without the presence and anointing of the Lord Jesus we would have no hope, but Jesus is real, and He answers prayer. No one has more compassion or mercy. Sometimes circumstances in our lives get desperate, and that is the time to lay hold of God as never before. Hook into God. That is the time to use our prayer language, the language of the Spirit, to plug into God's power and tune into His wavelength.

There is no reason why we should ever let anything unhook us from the presence and anointing of God. Nevertheless, it sometimes happens because we are human and prone to weakness and sin. Paul reminds us, however, that God sustains us in our weakness and gives us His strength. Referring to his "thorn in the flesh" that he prayed for the Lord to remove, Paul wrote:

> *And He said to me, "My grace is sufficient for you, for My strength is made perfect in weakness." Therefore most gladly I will rather boast in my infirmities, that the power of Christ may rest upon me. Therefore I take pleasure in infirmities, in reproaches, in needs, in persecutions, in distresses, for Christ's sake. For when I am weak, then I am strong* (2 Corinthians 12:9-10).

In Zechariah 4:6 God declares, "Not by might nor by power, but by My Spirit...."

In every situation, in every trial or tribulation or hardship, in every instance of life, the Holy Spirit stands ready to bless us, fill us, and take us to higher realms of glory and anointing. Each step we take, each new insight or revelation will help us see Jesus more clearly and more personally. What is required of us is passion—and hunger.

I know what it is to be in a desperate spot. Before our sons Aaron and Benjamin were born, Bonnie went through two extremely difficult and complicated pregnancies. At birth, both boys had severe physical problems and were not expected to survive. Our response was to pray. Bonnie and I prayed long and fervently. We prayed in tongues, connecting our spirits with the Spirit of God. The Lord was merciful. In both instances, our sons defied the doctors' predictions and made full recoveries, and both are hale and healthy young men today.

We are convinced beyond doubt of the value and power of speaking in tongues. It is the language of the Spirit, the prayer language that keeps us in the atmosphere of Heaven and helps us remain sensitive to the work of God's grace in our lives and to the healing and redemption provided for us by the cross of Christ. As we learn and practice praying in the Spirit, the Holy Spirit Himself molds inside us a heart through which spiritual gifts and spiritual fruit can flow easily.

Hunger for the things of the Spirit overcomes and confounds the wisdom of men. I remember ministering at Harvard University where many young adults, men and women in their early twenties, came in hungry for God. They were brilliant intellectuals—some of them already had one or two PhDs—but they had discovered that the intellectual realm alone could not free them. There they were, baptized in the Spirit, lying on the floor and speaking in tongues! One young man in the group was identified to me as the grandson of the late Ludwig Wittgenstein, an Austrian-born British philosopher highly regarded in the intellectual and academic worlds, and known for his absolute rejection of God or anything having to do with the spiritual. His grandson had come full circle; hungry for God and convinced of the inadequacy of intellect alone, he had embraced the faith his grandfather had rejected.

Do you have a passion for Jesus? Are you hungry for His presence, thirsty for His living water to flow out of your heart? Open up your mouth and let it come out and build yourself up in your most holy faith! The people who do great exploits will be those who know their God intimately and connect with Him in soul and spirit. The Lord is looking for a habitation, a place where He can dwell continually and manifest His glory. He wants to bring us into the realm of "greater works."

Greater Works Than These

The 14th chapter of John's Gospel contains one of the most awesome and incredible statements of Jesus recorded anywhere in the New Testament. It is the night before His crucifixion and Jesus is sharing His last hours with His disciples. Desiring to prepare them as best He can for what lies ahead, Jesus focuses on their need to understand who He is and to believe in Him:

> *Let not your heart be troubled; you believe in God, believe also in Me...I am the way, the truth, and the life. No one comes to the Father except through Me....He who has seen Me has seen the Father...Do you not believe that I am in the Father, and the Father in Me? The words that I speak to you I do not speak on My own authority; but the Father who dwells in Me does the works. Believe Me that I am in the Father and the Father in Me, or else believe Me for the sake of the works themselves* (John 14:1, 6,9b,10-11).

Five times Jesus uses the word "believe" in the context of His oneness with the Father and in reference to the works He has done. It is after these words that Jesus makes the statement that has such incredible implications for everyone who follows Him:

> *Most assuredly, I say to you, he who believes in Me, the works that I do he will do also; and greater works than these he will do, because I go to My Father. And whatever you ask in My name, that I will do, that the Father may be glorified in the Son. If you ask anything in My name, I will do it* (John 14:12-14).

As unbelievable as it sounds, Jesus promised that those who followed Him would do the same works that He did and, moreover, would do even greater works! How is that possible? The answer lies in the verses that immediately follow:

> *If you love Me, keep My commandments. And I will pray the Father, and He will give you another Helper, that He may abide with you forever—the Spirit of truth, whom the world cannot receive, because it neither sees Him nor knows Him; but you know Him, for He dwells with you and will be in you* (John 14:15-17).

Jesus was on the earth for only a few years and while here was limited to one place at one time. In contrast, however, the Holy Spirit would dwell in the hearts of believers as a permanent resident who would go with them everywhere and be with them always.

One of the most amazing things about Jesus' statement in verse 12 is the inclusiveness of His promise: The one who will do the same and greater works as Jesus will be "he who believes in Me." Entering into the greater works is not the exclusive privilege of ordained ministers or the "super-spiritual." It does not require a lot of education or theological training. It is not limited by race, nationality, gender, or even age. The only condition is to believe on Jesus Christ as Savior and Lord. Jesus has a vision for His people, a destiny for all who follow Him, that we should work in partnership with Him in doing His work and even "greater works" than those He did while on the earth.

Once I took a team with me to the nation of Haiti. During one meeting, hundreds of Haitians lined up waiting for me to walk by and lay hands on them and pray. I gathered my team together and asked them to raise their hands. They had no idea what I was going to do; I had said nothing to them beforehand. As they stood with hands raised, I prayed, "Lord, the anointing that You put on me, put on them." Then I instructed my team to go among the crowd and pray for them.

You should have seen the looks on their faces as my team members witnessed the power of God flowing through them in response to their prayers! In one case, a person who had been blind from birth received sight instantly! This was real! It had nothing to do with theology or education, but everything to do with impartation and the power of the name of Jesus. He is the King of glory and His name is truly above every other name.

There is nothing at all wrong with a good education or thorough academic preparation for ministry, but they are not a prerequisite for serving the Lord or for being filled and used by Him. Sometimes, depending on the circumstances or the person, too much learning can get in the way of an open heart. The apostle Paul, one of the most well-educated and brilliant intellectuals of his day, nevertheless spent several years (see Gal. 1:15-18) being discipled by the Holy Spirit before he was ready to fully undertake his apostolic calling. Although I have a university doctorate, the Lord led me to spend many years being mentored by some highly gifted people before the mantle of the anointing came for my mature ministry, and I am still learning all the time. The New Testament pattern is not so much education as spiritual impartation and an "apprenticeship" of serving and growing to maturity as preparation for the full mantle of ministry.

Jesus said that we would do the works He did, and what is even more astounding, that we would do greater works. What were the works of Jesus? He preached the gospel, healed the sick, opened the eyes of the blind, cast out demons, raised the dead, multiplied five loaves of bread and two fish to feed 5,000 people, and calmed storms with a single word.

All parents want their children to do better than they did. As our spiritual parent, Jesus wants us to enter into the greater works. That was part of the divine plan from the beginning. Jesus laid the foundation and we, through the Holy Spirit, are to build on what He began. That is our destiny. There is, of course, no way for us to fully understand this yet or to know exactly what form these greater works will take. One thing I can say with confidence is that we will be involved in some of the end-times works of Jesus to reach the nations of the world before He returns to establish His eternal kingdom.

Don't Disdain the Wilderness

There is nothing quite like being filled with the Spirit of God. Getting "zapped" by the Holy Ghost is fun! It's a wonderful feeling. We laugh and we praise and we worship and we say how wonderful the Holy Spirit is and how exciting it is to be led by the Spirit. Then, all of a sudden, we wake up one day and find that we're not where we thought we would be. Life takes on a little harder edge. Temptations are more frequent or stronger. We notice a dryness in our spirit, and we ask, "What happened? I thought I was following You, Holy Spirit, but it looks like I've ended up in the wilderness. Where are You, Lord? Where am I? Did I miss a turn somewhere along the way?"

One of the realities of life in the Spirit—in fact, it is a fundamental principle—is that we occasionally have to spend time in the wilderness. That is where we mature and where our greatest growth occurs. Moses spent 40 years in the wilderness of Midian before he was ready to lead the Israelites out of Egypt. David spent years hiding out in the wilderness and running from King Saul, who wanted to kill him, before the time came for him to become Israel's second and greatest king. Paul passed as many as fourteen years in preparation from the time of his conversion to Christ and the time he embarked fully on his apostolic mission. Jesus regularly sought out secluded or solitary places where He could pray.

We can take encouragement in our wilderness experiences from the example of Jesus Himself. Early on, at the very beginning of His public ministry, Jesus found Himself in the wilderness. It was not by accident.

> *Then Jesus, being filled with the Holy Spirit, returned from the Jordan and was led by the Spirit into the wilderness, being tempted for forty days by the devil. And in those days He ate nothing, and afterward, when they had ended, He was hungry.... Then Jesus returned in the power of the Spirit to Galilee, and news of Him went out through all the surrounding region. And He taught in their synagogues, being glorified by all* (Luke 4:1-2,14-15).

Jesus, filled with the Holy Spirit, was led into the wilderness *by* the Spirit, and later returned from the wilderness in the *power* of the Spirit. In between was a 40-day period of temptation and testing that shaped the direction and sharpened the focus of His public ministry.

Even the incarnate Son of God had to learn while He was on earth. In the wilderness, Jesus was enrolled in the school of the Spirit. For 40 days He fasted and prayed and did battle with satan, who sought to turn the Lord from His mission. At every temptation Jesus called on the Word of God and deflected every dart the enemy threw at Him. In the process, He defined how He would conduct His ministry of preaching, teaching, and healing.

Just as with His Son on earth, God our Father wants us to mature in the Holy Spirit. That is why from time to time He brings us into different seasons or levels of wilderness. It does not mean that we have missed His will or made a mistake or that He does not love us. Our wilderness periods are to help us grow into the anointing. Being in the wilderness does not mean that we have lost our connection to the Holy Spirit; He is still with us, just as He always is.

It is during such wilderness times as these that speaking in tongues is particularly valuable. Even when we have no idea what is going on, even when we have no clue what the Lord is doing with us, we can still use our prayer language to stay connected with Him at a level deeper than we can comprehend.

We need to be filled with the Holy Spirit, but that is only the beginning. Like Jesus, we need to enroll in the school of the Spirit and be discipled so that we can grow in the grace and knowledge of the Lord. He has provided the ideal place: the local church, with godly authority and godly shepherds. Be patient; maturity does not come overnight. Don't disdain the wilderness seasons of growing, because they help us put down strong roots of stability that can withstand the winds of wayward doctrines and the storms of adversity.

Ready and Waiting

The Lord is looking for hungry people through whom He can reveal His glory. Jesus said, "Blessed are those who hunger and thirst for righteousness, for they shall be filled" (Mt. 5:6). Second Chronicles 16:9a says, "For the eyes of the Lord run to and fro throughout the whole earth, to show Himself strong on behalf of those whose heart is loyal to Him." Being useful to God—being an instrument of His glory—does not require great learning or the ability to speak with eloquence. No seminary degree is necessary. All that God requires is a heart hungry for Him and a spirit willing and available for Him to fill and use.

One of the recurring lessons of Scripture is how the Lord uses humble instruments to accomplish great things. Moses had a stuttering problem, yet God empowered him to challenge the Egyptian pharaoh in his own palace. A simple scarlet cord hung from the window of Rahab's house in Jericho protected her and her family when the city fell to the Israelites, just as Rahab had protected the Israelite spies who had come to her. With a simple sling and five smooth stones David brought down a giant. Using nothing more than the jawbone of a donkey, Samson slew 1,000 Philistines. Jesus fed 5,000 people from a boy's simple lunch of five loaves of bread and two fish. A humble donkey bore on its back the King of kings as, only one week before He was crucified, He entered Jerusalem to the acclaim of the crowd.

Jesus' donkey ride into Jerusalem was a fulfillment of prophecy. The Gospel accounts of this event relate that Jesus sent some of His disciples to find a particular donkey and bring it for Him to ride on. Some scholars have suggested that Jesus had arranged this with the donkey's owner beforehand, but the Scriptures do not state or even imply such a thing. Throughout His life and public ministry Jesus relied on words of knowledge and words of wisdom that He received through the Holy Spirit.

I was leading a service in Minneapolis, Minnesota once when the Lord impressed on me that a couple was present whose little baby was terminally ill. The parents were unbelievers and had just received word that week of their child's condition. A neighbor had invited them to the meeting. They had never been to a service such as this one, but had come out of desperation.

As I stood up before 2,000 people, I realized I could not continue until I spoke the word that was on my heart. "There is a family here who lives on Pine Street. You have a child who is in desperate need. Where are you?" At that point the young couple screamed and came forward. I did not know them. I had never met them, yet they did live on Pine Street and their baby was seriously ill. That night God healed their baby.

The Lord gives words of knowledge; we are merely puny, humble servants of the King of Glory Himself. Through the Holy Spirit, Jesus knew that there was an owner who was willing to loan his donkey for the Master's use. If he had not been willing, the Lord would have found someone else who was. There were hundreds of donkeys in the city. What Jesus was looking for was availability.

More often than not we will not receive a full explanation of how or when or where the Lord is going to use us. He will simply say, "Get ready." For some reason, He is under the impression that He is the King, and He acts accordingly. He speaks, and our response is to say, "Yes, Sir." Obedience opens the pathway to blessing and prosperity in every area of life. The Lord will use those who are hungry for Him and willing to obey Him in all things.

Kathryn Kuhlman had one of the greatest evangelistic healing, signs, and wonders ministries of the twentieth century. She testified that the Lord had revealed to her that He had approached at least a dozen men, desiring to anoint them with that gift, but they had turned away from it. She said to Him, "Lord, however inadequate I am, however messed up my life has been, use me." He did use her in a mighty way. What made the difference? Kathryn Kuhlman was no different from any other believer except that she made herself completely available to the Lord.

It is the same way with us. If we make ourselves available to Him, the Lord will move in our lives through the simple things, and the simple things of God release the miracles of God. The pathway to the cross began with a donkey. The pathway to the glory of God revealed in and through us begins with a hunger and thirst for righteousness and a willingness to be available for the Lord's use, to be ready and waiting for the Lord to do with us as He will.

All the resources of Heaven are available to those who have trusted in Christ. He purchased our "ticket" with His own blood at the cross, and that ticket has paid for everything. The banquet is all laid out. It is time to step up to the table and eat. How hungry are you?

Chapter Nine

THE MELODY OF GOD

Hungry people are always on the lookout for that which will satisfy their hunger. Once they have acknowledged their craving, whether physical, emotional, or spiritual, feeding it becomes their first priority. Wherever they go and whatever they do, they have their nutritional "antenna" out, searching for even the tiniest signal that says, "Nourishment here." Hunger motivates them to diligently seek something they otherwise might not even think about.

In the natural world we are surrounded by an endless cacophony of signals and messages of all kinds. They are in the very air around us: radio waves, television signals, cellular telephone communications, satellite digital transmissions, and the like. We live in the midst of an electronic "cocoon" of broadcast transmissions, both verbal and nonverbal, both civilian and military. In a very literal sense, there is music in the air (not to mention newscasts, talk shows, commercials, and every other type of communication imaginable).

All of these are completely silent to us, however, unless we have an antenna to pick up the signal and a receiver to interpret the message. We turn on our radio or television, adjust the tuner to a particular frequency or channel, and we can find the news or music or program we desire. What we choose to watch or listen to is up to us, but the choice itself is often difficult because there are so many options. Depending on our choices, we can either nourish or starve our spirit.

In order to nourish our spirit, we have to put out our spiritual "antenna." Just as the physical air around us is full of signals and messages—"music in the air"—so the spiritual atmosphere is always filled with the melody of Heaven. In order to hear that melody we must have our spiritual antenna in place and tuned to the right frequency; otherwise we may pick up songs of darkness instead.

As Christians, we have two-way communication with the Lord that is on the air 24 hours a day, 7 days a week. The Holy Spirit is our divine "transceiver" through whom we both receive the melody of God and transmit our response. This kind of intimate interaction between God and us is the heart of both worship and prayer. When we are filled with the Spirit, He adjusts our "fine tuning" so that we are in perfect alignment with God's "frequency." The Spirit puts us on Heaven's "wavelength" so that we can pick up the "harmonic vibrations" of God. Our best response is to pray in the Spirit through speaking in tongues. By praying in the Spirit we sing back to God a melody in response to what we have heard from Him through the Spirit.

Make Melody in Your Heart

Praying in tongues helps us pick up the melody of the Lord. God has given each of us a song to sing; the challenge is learning what it is. It may be a Scripture, an extended message, or perhaps only a single word. Whatever our song, we need to sing it with joy and enthusiasm. Praying in the Spirit—in tongues—gets us in harmony with Heaven and in line to understand the will of God. The apostle Paul recognized the importance of making this connection, which is why he wrote to the believers in Ephesus:

Therefore do not be unwise, but understand what the will of the Lord is. And do not be drunk with wine, in which is dissipation; but be filled with the Spirit, speaking to one another in psalms and hymns and spiritual songs, singing and making melody in your heart to the Lord, giving thanks always for all things to God the Father in the name of our Lord Jesus Christ, submitting to one another in the fear of God (Ephesians 5:17-21).

On the Day of Pentecost, some scoffers accused the Spirit-baptized believers of being drunk. Even today, many Spirit-filled Christians often describe the experience as being "drunk in the Spirit." In reality, however, there is a great difference between being drunk and being in the Spirit. Paul described being drunk with wine as "dissipation," which means to expend wastefully in intemperate living or to be dissolute in the pursuit of pleasure. In another sense, the word means to allow something to spread thin or seep away. Drunkenness wastes gifts and talents. Alcohol is a depressant. Contrary to what many drinkers believe, intoxication dulls alertness and numbs sensibilities. It is impossible for someone under the influence of alcohol to perform at peak efficiency in any area.

Being filled with the Spirit, on the other hand, heightens our spiritual acuity. It increases our clarity of vision and understanding in both the spiritual and natural realms and raises our sensitivity to spiritual truth. That is why Paul placed such importance on it. The Holy Spirit, when He comes, brings to us an indescribable joy and a touch of the glory of Heaven. Being filled with the Spirit is not a one-time-only experience; the Lord's will is that we be filled over and over and over again. In Greek, the word for "be filled" in verse 18 represents *continuing action*: "be being filled with the Spirit." We are to experience continuous in-fillings. Our initial baptism in the Spirit is just the beginning, the first dose. We need to keep on being filled with the Spirit.

One result of that filling is that we will speak to one another "in psalms and hymns and spiritual songs." The filling of the Spirit, then, encourages and strengthens Christian fellowship. Another result is that we will sing and make melody in our hearts to the Lord. Being filled with the Spirit draws us into deeper and more intimate communion with our heavenly Father. Making melody in our hearts to God by praying in the Spirit helps us stay connected to an open Heaven. When we speak in tongues, we cooperate or move in harmony with the "waves" of God's glory. Speaking in tongues puts us in step with the mind and will of the Holy Spirit.

The more we pray in tongues, the more in tune we will be with the Holy Spirit, and the more in tune we are with the Holy Spirit, the more He will make our heart sing. We will pick up a melody of God that we cannot help but repeat. This will help protect our spirit because it keeps us focused on the right things. While one song is going on, it is difficult for us to sing another one. As long as we are singing the songs of heaven, of glory, of healing, of restoration, of the prophetic anointing, and of the end-time restoration of the Lord, we won't be singing songs of darkness from the enemy. The world around us is full of those, too. Singing the melody of God will help us follow Paul's admonition to "seek those things which are above, where Christ is, sitting at the right hand of God. Set your mind on things above, not on things on the earth" (Col. 3:1b-2).

Getting in tune with Heaven means setting our minds and spirits on the things of God, things that align with His character and nature. Again, in the words of Paul:

Finally, brethren, whatever things are true, whatever things are noble, whatever things are just, whatever things are pure, whatever things are lovely, whatever things are of good report, if there is any virtue and if there is anything praiseworthy—meditate on these things (Philippians 4:8).

One of the keys to hearing and singing God's melody in our hearts is to get into the habit of "giving thanks always for all things to God the Father in the name of our Lord Jesus Christ" (Eph. 5:20). A thankless heart or an ungrateful spirit will drown out the melody of God. The more thankful we are, the more we will open the door of God's blessings for ourselves and our families. Ingratitude, grumbling, and complaining, on the other hand, will make us more susceptible to demonic influence ruling over our situation.

Be filled with the Spirit. Pray in tongues. Make melody in your heart to the Lord, and bring in the atmosphere of glory.

Harmonizing With Heaven

Picking up the melody of God is like becoming a spiritual tuning fork. A tuning fork is a two-pronged instrument made out of a very pure metal that when struck vibrates at a precise frequency, producing a pure pitch with no overtones. If a vibrating tuning fork is brought into contact with a hard surface, such as a table, and another tuning fork that is not vibrating is also brought into contact with that surface, the second tuning fork will pick up the vibrations of the first one and begin vibrating in synchronization with it.

When we pray in the Spirit we are like that second tuning fork. The first fork hums with the vibrant harmonies of God, which are then transmitted through the table (the Holy Spirit). As we connect with the Spirit in prayer, we begin to "hum" in sympathetic resonance to the divine melody. Nothing feels better mentally or spiritually than to resonate "in synch" with God—to feel His "vibes"—or in the words of that classic Beach Boys' song, to pick up those "good vibrations."

To resonate with someone means to relate harmoniously or to be in harmony with him or her. Another meaning is to agree. When we resonate with the melody of God, it means we are in harmony with Him and in agreement with His will. We are "in synch" with One to whom everything belongs and for whom nothing is impossible.

Love is the melody of God. The main theme of His song is the blood of Jesus shed at Calvary, and it has many variations. Jesus was "struck" for us and the vibration of His death resonates louder than any other vibration in our lives. The blood of Jesus speaks for us. God's love song sets our spirits humming in harmony with the One who was struck on our behalf.

A vibrating tuning fork gives off a tone that is very soft and hard to hear. A hard surface amplifies the tone so that it becomes plainly audible. In the same way, the Holy Spirit amplifies the melody of God so that we can hear it and sing along. We must be quiet, however, and listen to hear God's love song. Psalm 46:10a says, "Be still, and know that I am God." He wants to release us into peace without fear, into a love that is confident in letting go of our anxieties and dependence upon our own good works, to rest in His mercy and grace. Once we let go of our own song, we are able to pick up the Lord's song from Heaven and sing in harmony with Him.

Harmonizing With the Body

S inging the melody of God does more than just put us in harmony with Him vertically; it also harmonizes us horizontally with other believers, particularly those in the same church fellowship. One great hallmark of the Holy Spirit's presence is unity in the body. From the beginning, the Lord has desired that His people be in harmony as a corporate body being built up in love, who acknowledge one Lord and speak with one voice by one Spirit.

On Monday, January 1, 1739, John Wesley, his brother Charles, and a few other associates gathered for a love feast at Fetter Lane in England, together with about 60 other believers. The meeting continued far into the night. As John Wesley recorded in his journal:

> At about 3:00 in the morning, as we were continu-
> ing instant in prayer, the power of God came might-
> ily upon us in so much that many cried out for
> exceeding joy and many fell to the ground. As soon
> as we were recovered a little from that awe and
> amazement at the presence of His Majesty, we broke
> out with one voice, "We praise Thee, oh God, we
> acknowledge Thee to be the Lord."

Notice that when the presence of the Lord came down, Wesley and the other believers began to praise God "with one voice." They were in harmony not only with the melody of God, but also with each other.

Harmony within the Body of Christ is absolutely essen-tial if the Church of the new millennium is to be effective in reaching the nations with the gospel. The common denomina-tor that unites us all is the melody of God: His love song of the shed blood of Jesus. Paul knew that song and described it as

"Jesus Christ and Him crucified." We as the church must sing that song in perfect harmony if we want to be sure the world will understand. If we are divided or confused or singing different songs or even different parts of the same song, how can we expect anyone to respond to our message? "For if the trumpet makes an uncertain sound, who will prepare for battle?" (1 Cor. 14:8)

Amos 3:3 asks, "Can two walk together, unless they are agreed?" The writer of Ecclesiastes points out the strength and power of a unified group over an individual:

Two are better than one, because they have a good reward for their labor. For if they fall, one will lift up his companion. But woe to him who is alone when he falls, for he has no one to help him up. Again, if two lie down together, they will keep warm; but how can one be warm alone? Though one may be overpowered by another, two can withstand him. And a threefold cord is not quickly broken (Ecclesiastes 4:9-12).

God has always desired His people to live in harmony and relate in love. Today the Lord is calling His Church to walk with Him and agree with Him. Through the Holy Spirit He has tuned us to the melody of God, and the primary way we manifest our harmony is through corporate prayer. As we walk with the Lord both individually and corporately, the Holy Spirit will assist and enable us to agree (harmonize) with one another as we walk together.

Through the years the Church has tried all sorts of things and undertaken all kinds of programs to try to get together on theology, doctrine, and ministry. Corporate prayer is the best way for a church to harmonize, both within itself and with other fellowships, but it must be Spirit-filled, Spirit-led corporate prayer. Centering our efforts on the ideas or agendas of men will never work. John Wesley and the others simply gathered in the presence of the Lord, harmonizing together, waiting on God until He came.

Derek Prince has said that any prayer not led of the Holy Spirit will not touch God. If what he says is true, it reveals just how important the Holy Spirit is to everything we do. He prays for us at all times, and particularly when we don't know what to say:

> *Likewise the Spirit also helps in our weaknesses. For we do not know what we should pray for as we ought, but the Spirit Himself makes intercession for us with groanings which cannot be uttered. Now He who searches the hearts knows what the mind of the Spirit is, because He makes intercession for the saints according to the will of God* (Romans 8:26-27).

"Groanings which cannot be uttered"—that's the way the Spirit of God prays. Corporate prayer in the language of the Spirit harmonizes the Church and connects it to the conduit through which the power and anointing of God flow. Praying in the Spirit is aside from the dynamic of evangelism and salvation proclaimed in a language that can be clearly understood in order that the lost may see the light of Christ and come in. The two go together. Corporate prayer is the vehicle through which the Lord empowers His Church to proclaim the gospel with authority.

Spiritual Voice Lessons

In many ways, learning to sing in the spiritual is like learning to sing in the natural. The first things beginning voice students learn are the mechanics of proper singing: erect posture, deep breathing, relaxation of throat, jaws, and vocal cords, and correct tone placement utilizing the resonant chambers of the mouth and sinus cavities. All of these must be in place if the student's goal of becoming a good singer is to be realized. It is very similar in the spirit realm. If we wish to sing well the melody of God, we must learn to place ourselves in the proper *posture* of spiritual prayer, *breathe* deeply of the breath of Heaven and of the Spirit (the Greek word *pneuma*, which means "spirit," also means "breath"), relax our spirits to rest in the Lord, and *place* our song in such a way that we can resonate with the music of glory.

It is the same with praying in the Spirit as with singing in the natural: The more we practice, the better we will get and the stronger we will become. The only way to increase our capacity is through exercise. If we want to become skilled singers of God's song—the melody of love—we have to spend time practicing our spiritual voice lessons. As Jude says, "But you, beloved, building yourselves up on your most holy faith, praying in the Holy Spirit, keep yourselves in the love of God..." (Jude 20-21a).

Praying in the Spirit consistently will lead to breakthrough in every area of life, and we will find ourselves greatly strengthened in our "inner man." Every weak place, every doubting place, every discouraged place, every fearful place, every broken place, every oppressed place will be built up and strengthened.

Any skill or capacity will atrophy from disuse. Many Christians have weak and flaccid prayer "muscles" because they do not exercise them enough. Considering all the challenges that face us as the end-times generation in the new millennium, we cannot afford to be out of condition spiritually. There is too much at stake. It's high time for all of us to get into the spiritual "gym" and exercise our prayer language and build our capacity to breathe the breath of Heaven and sing God's love song with all our might.

Too often we tend to relegate our prayer language to some little religious corner of our lives, or squeeze it in between songs at church. How little attention we sometimes give to such an awesome gift! Whenever we pray in the Spirit, the Holy Spirit Himself is praying for us and with us, interceding on our behalf. Who can pray better than He can? Who knows our hearts, our minds, and our needs better than the One who abides continually in us? Who knows our gifts and capacities better than the One who gave them to us? For most of us, our lives are too fast-paced for us to get by with prayers that are nothing more than 30-second spiritual "sound bites." We need regular spiritual voice lessons to train us to sing God's song, and consistent exercise to build up our prayer "muscle."

Among the primary themes of God's love song is to exalt the Lord. His song can be many things. God's love song always exalts the Lord, but it can take many different forms. When we pray in the Spirit, we will not always sing the song the same way. We have to learn to just let it flow as the Spirit leads us. Sometimes our song will be like water tumbling down over rocks, very intense and pointed and with a nature of warfare and aggressive faith behind it. At other times it will be like a gentle flowing stream.

As we learn to flow in the Spirit, the Lord oftentimes will give revelation to our minds. We may see peoples' faces or the impressions of nations or international events or other prophetic things. If we simply stay in the flow and don't try to understand or figure these things out with our own minds, the Lord will increase our capacity and fill us to overflowing like a mighty river pouring through us to do His work. It is much easier (and wiser) for Him to pray the agenda and for us to simply give voice to it.

As we saw in Chapter four, praying in the Spirit is an avenue by which we may come to know the deep things of God, spiritual truths and realities that cannot be known or understood by human wisdom alone. Paul told the Corinthian believers that human wisdom and imagination could not conceive the things that God had prepared for those who love Him, but that the Holy Spirit had revealed them to believers (1 Cor. 2:9-10). The Holy Spirit gives us knowledge of those things that God has freely given us (see 1 Cor. 2:12).

Such knowledge is not only beyond the comprehension of unbelievers, but even seems foolish to them. "But the natural man does not receive the things of the Spirit of God, for they are foolishness to him; nor can he know them, because they are spiritually discerned" (1 Cor. 2:14). Our capacity to understand spiritual things is not because the Holy Spirit has "supercharged" our human minds, but because we have been given the mind of Christ. "For 'who has known the mind of the Lord that he may instruct Him?' But we have the mind of Christ" (1 Cor. 2:16).

Because we have the mind of Christ, once we begin praying in the Spirit we will start to understand more and more of what God has freely given to us, to our families, and to our churches. As we pray in the Spirit, the Lord will give us spiritual wisdom and insight, and we will be able to "sing with understanding" (1 Cor. 14:15b) the melody of God.

My Sheep Hear My Voice

If learning to "give thanks always for all things" is one key to singing the melody of God, another key, even more important, is learning how to hear and recognize the voice of

144

God. We cannot sing a song we do not know, and we cannot learn a song that we cannot hear. One of the roles of the Holy Spirit in our lives is to teach us to hear and follow the voice of our Master, the Lord Jesus Christ.

One day Jesus was surrounded by Jewish religious leaders who were at odds with Him over some of His teaching. As they did often, they tested Him in an effort to trap Him with His own words.

> Then the Jews surrounded Him and said to Him, "How long do You keep us in doubt? If You are the Christ, tell us plainly." Jesus answered them, "I told you, and you do not believe. The works that I do in My Father's name, they bear witness of Me. But you do not believe, because you are not of My sheep, as I said to you. My sheep hear My voice, and I know them, and they follow Me" (John 10:24-27).

In the natural realm, sheep know the voice of their shepherd and will follow no other. Even if several flocks of sheep are mingled together at one pasturing place, all a shepherd has to do is call out and his sheep will immediately separate themselves from the others and come to him. Those who are not his sheep will pay no attention.

Jesus said, "I am the good shepherd; and I know My sheep, and am known by My own" (Jn. 10:14). For those of us who believe, Jesus is our Shepherd and He knows us. Jesus knows everything about us: who we are, where we came from, our past, our present, and our future. He knows our likes and our dislikes, our joys and our sorrows, our hopes and our fears. He knows all our best points and all our worst points. Jesus knows us and speaks to us and we are able to hear and recognize His voice because He is the Good Shepherd who laid down His life for His sheep.

In John 10:27 Jesus describes three characteristics of His sheep: They hear His voice, He knows each of them, and they follow Him. This is in sharp contrast to Jesus' words in Matthew 7:22-23: "Many will say to Me in that day, 'Lord, Lord, have we not prophesied in Your name, cast out demons in Your name, and done many wonders in Your name?' And then I will declare to them, 'I never knew you; depart from Me, you who practice lawlessness!'"

The word for lawlessness in this passage is *anomia*. It comes from *nomos* signifying "food for grazing animals." Jesus equates obeying His words to having intimate knowledge of Him. He said, "Behold, I stand at the door and knock. If anyone hears My voice and opens the door (of his heart), I will come in to him and dine with him, and he with Me" (Rev. 3:20). Those who refuse to "eat" the words of the Shepherd are not His sheep!

Our destiny in Christ is to hear His voice in this hour and follow Him, to begin to resonate with the frequency of Heaven. When we pray in the Spirit we say the same thing as the voice that speaks from Heaven, letting the Word of God bubble up out of us as a living river for the nations of the earth.

The voice of the Shepherd, the spirit of prophecy, and the song of the sheep are closely intertwined. Both Ezekiel the prophet and John the Revelator were given the words of the Lord to eat. As they did so, both experienced His Word to be as sweet as honey in their mouths. In Ezekiel 2:8, God commands the prophet, "But you, son of man, hear what I say to you. Do not be rebellious like that rebellious house; open your mouth and eat what I give you." Ezekiel then saw a scroll written on both sides, after which God said, "Son of man, eat what you find; eat this scroll, and go, speak to the house of Israel" (Ezek. 3:1). John had a similar experience in Revelation 10:9-11.

An angel handed John a little book and said to him, "Take and eat it" and, after John had eaten the book, "You must prophesy..."

At the close of the Sermon on the Mount, right after His words about the danger of not knowing Him, Jesus makes it clear that obedience to the Word of God is the foundation for a secure life: "Therefore whoever hears these sayings of Mine, and does them, I will liken him to a wise man who built his house upon the rock; and the rain descended, the floods came, and the winds blew and beat on that house; and it did not fall, for it was founded on the rock" (Mt. 7:24-25).

Knowing Christ is the first criterion for obeying Him. Everything else builds from that. The Holy Spirit brings us into knowledge of the Lord by revealing to us the things God has freely given us, things that are known only through spiritual discernment. Obedience brings intimacy with God. The more intimate we are with God, the better we will be able to hear His love song, and the better we can hear His love song, the better we will be able to sing it in harmony with Him.

Stay in Tune

Tongues is one of the great mysteries of God. I don't understand it, but I'm going to continue to speak in tongues because it is a pathway of glory. The Lord is in the midst of doing something awesome in His Church, and He is inviting every one of us to participate. We each have a melody in our hearts, a harmony with God that is uniquely ours, and He wants us to sing it. The more we sing, the more He will begin to reveal some of the mystery. As we get in harmony with God, making melody in our hearts, He will release more of the spirit of revelation, with words of wisdom, words of knowledge, even prophetic songs.

Whatever song the Lord gives us, we need to take it up and sing because it connects us to the heart and mind of the Father. Praying in the Spirit and making melody in our hearts will allow us to see more of the glory atmosphere around us. It will be permeated with miracles: Healings and restoration miracles will come forth even more than before. Singing the melody of God charges the atmosphere around us. As we become conscious of that charged atmosphere and walk in it, we will begin to speak prophetically and creatively in a way that will help change people's lives.

Although we can each sing our individual song, corporate prayer with other believers is where our harmony can best be heard. That is why it is important for us to stay connected and active with a Bible-believing, Spirit-filled, and Spirit-led church. Otherwise we run the risk of getting out of tune. Even in a large orchestra, one instrument out of tune will stand out and destroy the harmony of the rest of the group. If we insist on going it alone, we have no way to know for sure if our "instrument" is in proper tune or if we are still singing the right melody.

We need regular fellowship with other believers in the Lord's house to make sure we stay in tune with the heart of God. The writer of Hebrews was very clear on this point:

> *Let us hold fast the confession of our hope without wavering, for He who promised is faithful. And let us consider one another in order to stir up love and good works, not forsaking the assembling of ourselves together, as is the manner of some, but exhorting one another, and so much the more as you see the Day approaching* (Hebrews 10:23-25).

The "confession of our hope" is another way of describing God's melody in our heart. When we assemble together regularly as believers, it is easier for all of us to pick up the melody of the Lord. Together we can sing songs of deliverance, songs of healing, songs of wisdom and knowledge, and then we can take those deliverance, healing, and knowledge situations with us wherever we go. The melody of God is transportable, but we need regular fellowship—with God and with each other—to make sure we stay in tune and sing the song correctly.

Jesus said, "As the Father has sent Me, I also send you" (Jn. 20:21b). Wherever He went during His earthly ministry, Jesus never simply accepted the atmosphere as He found it. He brought His tune into every situation and changed the atmosphere. Into an atmosphere of death He sang life; into an atmosphere of disease He sang healing; into an atmosphere of despair He sang hope. Jesus sang His tune into every situation; He did not allow that situation to sing its own tune or to call out the melody.

As children of God we are all kings and priests. Kings speak with authority and priests bring the connection of God into a situation. When we connect with the mind and heart of the Lord, He will give us glory songs that we can sing into the situations around us. God has given us the opportunity and privilege to be His instruments through whom He will transform people's lives. This is an awesome but wonderful responsibility that calls for humility on our part as well as a deep sense of dependence, both on Christ and on each other. We must make certain that we are singing the right melody and that we are singing it clearly. This is why we must stay connected with the Word of God, the leading of the Holy Spirit, and the fellowship of other believers. If we are to sing the melody of God correctly, we must allow Him to use these things to restore and transform us.

Chapter Ten

RESTORED AND TRANSFORMED

One day my wife Bonnie was out on one of her "power walks." Bonnie is very serious when it comes to her exercise. She concentrates on keeping her cardio-vascular rate up so she can get a good workout, and also uses these outings for intense alone times with God. At the same time she exercises her body she also exercises her spirit, speaking in tongues and wrestling to "lay hold" of God as much as she can. So, she really gets into it.

On this particular day Bonnie was about halfway through her four mile walk when she decided to head through the woods near our home instead of taking the road as she usually did. It was cold and Bonnie was just barreling along, praying about an upcoming conference. As she came up over a grassy rise she saw a butterfly sitting in the grass, waving its wings slowly in the cold air. She almost stepped on it. For some reason, Bonnie stopped long enough to pick it up, then kept going. She was afraid she would hurt it by holding it, so she put it on her arm and finished her walk.

To make a long story short, that butterfly stayed with Bonnie for the next 24 hours before it finally flew away. Right after her workout, Bonnie showered and dressed, and the butterfly was with her the whole time. As she stood in front of her mirror, the butterfly rested on her hair. As Bonnie then began fixing her hair, the butterfly flew off and landed on the mirror. When Bonnie looked closer in the mirror to apply her makeup, she noticed little flecks of gold on her forehead right where the butterfly had been sitting. Immediately she thought of Paul's words in Second Corinthians:

> *Now the Lord is the Spirit; and where the Spirit of the Lord is, there is liberty. But we all, with unveiled face, beholding as in a mirror the glory of the Lord, are being transformed into the same image from glory to glory, just as by the Spirit of the Lord* (2 Corinthians 3:17-18).

Paul was talking about our being transformed into the image of the glorious Lord Jesus. The Spirit of God is transforming us "from glory to glory"—from earthly glory to heavenly glory—into the very likeness of Christ. That transformation takes place within the context of real life.

Manifesting the Life of Jesus

Change is an inevitable part of life, yet there is something about the human soul that has difficulty going through metamorphosis without suffering. I think that the process by which a caterpillar becomes a butterfly provides a good analogy of how God works to conform us to the image of Christ and transform us. A caterpillar spins a cocoon around itself and is lost to the view of the world for a time. Outwardly, that cocoon appears mysterious, perhaps even ugly, but inside a wonderful change is taking place.

Before the caterpillar's transformation into a butterfly is complete, however, it must struggle its way out of the cocoon. Without the struggle the butterfly will die. As it fights to break out of the cocoon, the butterfly's movements force fluid into its wings so that when it is finally free it is strong and can fly and care for itself. Only through struggle does a butterfly fulfill its destiny and release its full glory.

As believers, we need to look at our struggles the same way. The "spirit man" in each of us is eternal, and it is that part of us that the Lord is conforming to the image of Christ. He is training us for eternity. No matter how bad circumstances may get, this life is only temporary. In the light of forever, our present difficulties are insignificant. If we let them, however, our struggles will serve to strengthen and mature us and help us fulfill the destiny God has for us. The pressures of life can squeeze us until the glory of the Lord that is inside us comes out.

Paul knew that it was in the crucible of daily living that the KIngdom of God would be made manifest in us:

> But we have this treasure in earthen vessels, that the excellence of the power may be of God and not of us. We are hard-pressed on every side, yet not crushed; we are perplexed, but not in despair; persecuted, but not forsaken; struck down, but not destroyed—always carrying about in the body the dying of the Lord Jesus, that the life of Jesus also may be manifested in our body. For we who live are always delivered to death for Jesus' sake, that the life of Jesus also may be manifested in our mortal flesh. (2 Corinthians 4:7-11).

This "treasure" that we have in the "earthen vessels" of our bodies is the Holy Spirit, the very breath and life of God, who saturates us so that the rays of His glory shine through in the same way that Moses' face shone after meeting with God on the mountain. With the words, "always carrying about in the body the dying of the Lord Jesus, that the life of Jesus also may be manifested in our body," Paul identifies a very real Kingdom principle. As believers we carry "the dying of the Lord Jesus" everywhere; our very lives are testimonies to His death and what it accomplished for us.

At the same time, we manifest the resurrection life of Jesus in our bodies by the way we live each day and by how we respond to the challenges and struggles that come with being human. Often we have little control over the tests, difficulties, and obstacles that come our way, but we do have control over the attitude we take toward them. Nothing happens to a child of God by accident or without God's knowledge or permission. All the things we experience that cause us difficulty, humble us, or test our patience are part of the Spirit's work of molding us into the image of the Lord Jesus Christ. What we must always keep preeminent in our minds as we live in the real world is that by those very things the resurrection power of Jesus will manifest in us to His glory, transforming us more and more into royal children, prepared to assume our rightful place as heirs of God's Kingdom.

We need to ask ourselves where our daily focus of life is. One of the things that the Lord wants to do in us is to change our day-to-day perspective emotionally, physically, and spiritually so that we see the world and our lives not from our point of view but from His. Our natural tendency is to focus primarily on what our senses detect as "real"—that which we can see, hear, smell, taste, and touch. As tangible as they appear, those things are only temporary because they belong to the physical realm, which is passing away. We should fix our eyes on the things that are unseen, for they are eternal.

Paul puts the entire matter into perspective for us with these words:

Therefore we do not lose heart. Even though our outward man is perishing, yet the inward man is being renewed day by day. For our light affliction, which is but for a moment, is working for us a far more exceeding and eternal weight of glory, while we do not look at the things which are seen, but at the things which are not seen. For the things which are seen are temporary, but the things which are not seen are eternal (2 Corinthians 4:16-18).

Our physical bodies are temporary and will pass away, but our spirits are eternal. The Holy Spirit in us connects us inseparably to the resurrection life of Jesus. Regularly praying in the Spirit helps keep the connection strong and secure. Day by day, little by little, He is transforming us into the image of Christ's glory. That image shines through the temporary earthen vessels that contain it so that a world with its eyes fixed only on that which can be seen can be drawn to focus on that which is eternal.

In Good Company

Paul said, "We who live are always delivered to death for Jesus' sake." Daily life for Paul and other believers of his generation was characterized by frequent oppression, opposition, and persecution. Christians were routinely crucified or thrown into the arena to be killed by wild animals. Many more had their belongings confiscated and their property seized. At one point, many Christians in or near Rome were tied to posts, covered with pitch, and set on fire to serve as lampposts to light the highway at night. In spite of this persecution, Christians of the first century remained faithful and steadfast overall and by the end of the century had spread the gospel throughout the Roman Empire.

Whether we interpret it literally, as in martyrdom, or figuratively, as in a daily dying to self and absolute surrender to Jesus, Paul's statement is just as true today as it was when he made it. In our sufferings and struggles for Jesus' sake we are in good company. Through the Spirit of God we are inseparably connected with those saints who have gone before us. As the writer of Hebrews encourages us:

Therefore we also, since we are surrounded by so great a cloud of witnesses, let us lay aside every weight, and the sin which so easily ensnares us, and let us run with endurance the race that is set before us, looking unto Jesus, the author and finisher of our faith, who for the joy that was set before Him endured the cross, despising the shame, and has sat down at the right hand of the throne of God (Hebrews 12:1-2).

A great cloud of witnesses—those who have gone before—are now seated in the stadium, as it were, watching us run the race. They have already been where we are and they urge us on. Most of us will never be called on to endure what they endured, but when we go through tough times it is encouraging to remember that we are not alone in our struggle. The same power that carried them through is available to us because we have the same Spirit. As the mountain that we must climb looms before us, we can draw upon the same reservoir of truth, power, and anointing to give us the perseverance we need to climb to the top, plant our flag, and proclaim, "I have overcome!" Once we learn to think of ourselves not as loners but as members of a common family, a great, worldwide, centuries-spanning company with a common faith and common challenges, the difficulties in our own lives don't seem as threatening as they did before.

Just as in a physical race, we may start out in the spirit all pumped up and ready to go. We take off at a steady pace, really feeling good. Somewhere along the way, however, our energy begins to flag. Our sugar is gone, our side is hurting, our feet ache. Suddenly, we don't feel so powerful anymore. The fun and excitement are gone, and we feel like dropping out of the race to sit on the sidelines and read the newspaper. It seems as though we don't have any breath left and can't possibly take another step. We sure could use a power bar right about now!

This is what athletes call "hitting the wall." It's important to persevere, however, because just beyond the wall is the place of second wind, a renewal of energy and endurance that will take us to the finish line. The problem is that too many of us stop when we hit the wall, rather than pressing on beyond it to the place of second wind. The Spirit of God is our wind, the divine "breath" that enables us to go the distance. Along the way we can help ourselves to many spiritual "power bars" to boost our energy level. The Word of God is a power bar. Prayer is a power bar. The blood of Jesus is a power bar. The anointing of the Spirit is a power bar. Speaking in tongues is a power bar. Fellowship with other believers is a power bar. All of these help us stay connected to the Lord and to each other as we "run with endurance the race that is set before us."

Can These Bones Live?

R estoration and transformation lie at the heart of God's desire for His people. The gifts and calling of God are without repentance. All His promises are true and will be fulfilled to the last letter. What God has begun He will finish; what He has willed shall come to pass. No matter how many times we falter or turn away or become distracted, God will never give up on us or abandon us. He is determined to bring us into the fullness of everything He has promised.

God's purpose and power to restore and transform His people is revealed plainly and graphically in chapters 36 and 37 of the Book of Ezekiel. The nation of Israel was desolate. Centuries of continued rebellion and disobedience toward God had brought His judgment. The empire of Babylon had conquered the land and many of the Jews were in exile. Jerusalem was in ruins and the temple destroyed. By their own self-assessment, they mourned, "Our bones are dry, our hope is lost, and we ourselves are cut off!" (Ezek. 37:11b) They had been brought lower than low.

In Ezekiel chapter 36, however, God begins to speak line upon line of restoration and blessing that He is going to manifest in His people. It hasn't happened yet, but God's words are as certain of fulfillment as if they have already come to pass. "For all the promises of God in Him are Yes, and in Him Amen..." (2 Cor. 1:20).

Following this revelation to Ezekiel of the blessings He is going to bring to Israel, God gives the prophet a powerful vision of a valley filled with desiccated human bones. As Ezekiel gazed upon the scene, the Lord asked, "Son of man, can these bones live?" (Ezek. 37:3b) Ezekiel knows that in the natural it is impossible, but also that God is powerful and true to His eternal covenant. The prophet answers, "O Lord God, You know" (Ezek. 37:3c). God spoke to the prophet once more:

Again He said to me, "Prophesy to these bones, and say to them, 'O dry bones, hear the word of the Lord! Thus says the Lord God to these bones: "Surely I will cause breath to enter into you, and you shall live. I will put sinews on you and bring

flesh upon you, cover you with skin and put breath
in you; and you shall live. Then you shall know that
I am the Lord" ' " (Ezekiel 37:4-6).

As Ezekiel obeys and begins to prophesy, the river of the
Spirit of God flows through him with great authority and
power. Line by line, layer by layer, piece by piece, these dry
bones come together. The bones form themselves into complete skeletons, sinews and flesh cover them, and finally, the
breath of God animates the bodies and brings them to life,
standing in the valley as a mighty army.

At one time or another just about all of us have been in
our own valley where, like Ezekiel's dry bones, we have felt
forgotten, lifeless, and useless. Many people live in that valley
every day. Whenever we find ourselves in such a place, the
good news is that God says to us, "I will."

The Revealed "Will" of God

Have you ever heard someone pray, "Thy will be done..."
as if they are certain that it is God's will to desert his
people, leaving them to suffer and struggle through on their
own with every kind of difficulty hopelessly overtaking them?
Nothing could be further from the truth. In chapters 36 and 37
of Ezekiel, God promises no fewer than 20 times that He
"will" do certain things for His people. He sets forth 20 initiatives for deliverance, restoration, and well-being. In addition, He speaks 11 initiatives for the land itself and eight
initiatives for the will of the people.

Although the promises contained in these chapters refer
specifically to the physical land and nation of Israel as well as
His covenant people who were to live there, God never
changes. His ways and His will for His people and the land
they inhabit remain constant. God's decision to bless Israel

was not because Israel was deserving, but because of who God is. "Therefore say to the house of Israel, 'Thus says the Lord God: "I do not do this for your sake, O house of Israel, but for My holy name's sake, which you have profaned among the nations wherever you went" ' " (Ezek. 36:22).

The same promise applies to us. God's will for all of us as believers, and for the lands we inhabit, whether the United States or any other nation, is that the land may flourish in order that He might be a blessing to His people and bring glory to His name. Realizing this will help instill confidence and clarity in us concerning how to pray for our nation and what to expect God to do.

Eleven Initiatives in the Will of God for the *Land* of Israel:

1. "I will turn to you" (look on you with favor)—Ezekiel 36:9.

2. "You shall (will) be tilled and sown"—Ezekiel 36:9.

3. "I will multiply men upon you"—Ezekiel 36:10.

4. "I will multiply on you...beast" (livestock)—Ezekiel 36:11.

5. "I will make you inhabited as in former times"—Ezekiel 36:11.

6. "I will do better for you than at your beginnings" (prosper them)—Ezekiel 36:11.

7. "You shall (will) know that I am the Lord"—Ezekiel 36:11.

8. "I will cause men to walk on you, My people Israel"—Ezekiel 36:12.

9. "You shall (will) be their (Israel's) inheritance"—Ezekiel 36:12.

10. "No more shall (will) you bereave them of children"—Ezekiel 36:12.

11. "I Will sanctify My great name" (show its holiness)—Ezekiel 36:23.

Twenty Initiatives in the Will of God for *His* People:

1. He will bring us home: "For I will take you from among the nations...and bring you into your own land"—Ezekiel 36:24.

2. He will refresh and wash us: "Then I will sprinkle clean water on you, and you shall be clean"—Ezekiel 36:25a.

3. He will separate us from sin: "I will cleanse you from all your filthiness and from all your idols"—Ezekiel 36:25b.

4. He will transform our mind, will, and emotions: "I will give you a new heart and put a new spirit within you"—Ezekiel 36:26a.

5. He will give us rebirth: "I will take the heart of stone out of your flesh and give you a heart of flesh"—Ezekiel 36:26b.

6. He will put His ways in us: "I will put My Spirit within you and cause you to walk in My statutes, and you will keep My judgments and do *them*—Ezekiel 36:27.

7. He will cause us to know and serve Him: "You shall be My people, and I will be your God"—Ezekiel 36:28b.

8. He will forgive and deliver us: "I will deliver you from all your uncleannesses"—Ezekiel 36:29a.

9. He will restore our resources (seed for producing harvest): "I will call for the grain and multiply it"—Ezekiel 36:29b.

10. He will keep us from lack: "I will...bring no famine upon you"—Ezekiel 36:29c.

11. He will feed us and take away the shame of being forsaken by God: "And I will multiply the fruit of your trees and the increase of your fields, so that you need never again bear the reproach of famine among the nations"—Ezekiel 36:30.

12. He will drive satan off of our inheritance: "I will also enable you to dwell in the cities"—Ezekiel 36:33b.

13. He will perform His word: "I, the Lord...have spoken it, and I will do it"—Ezekiel 36:36b.

14. He will hear our prayers: "I will also let the house of Israel inquire of Me..."—Ezekiel 36:37b.

15. He will bring people into our lives to add blessing and strength: "I will increase their men like a flock. Like a flock offered as holy sacrifices, like the flock at Jerusalem on its feast days, so shall the ruined cities be filled with flocks of men..."—Ezekiel 36:37c-38. (During the time of sacrifices for the feasts in Jerusalem the streets were filled with sheep!)

16. He will revive us: "I will cause breath to enter into you..."—Ezekiel 37:5b.

17. He will strengthen and enable us: "I will put sinews on you and bring flesh upon you"—Ezekiel 37:6a.

18. He will give us inspiration and authority: "I will...put breath in you; and you shall live"—Ezekiel 37:6c.

19. He will bring us into His destiny: "I will...bring you into the land of Israel"—Ezekiel 37:12b.

20. He will anoint us with His Spirit: "I will put My Spirit in you, and you shall live..."—Ezekiel 37:14a.

As Ezekiel received the revelation of God's will for the land and people, he had a very important part to play. Three times, in verse 4,9, and 12 of chapter 37 the Lord commands him to "prophesy" to the bones—to proclaim aloud what God had promised. In each case, as Ezekiel obeys, God brings to completion each phase of His work of restoring and transforming His people. First, the bones come together, bone to bone, and flesh and sinews cover them. Second, God breathes His breath into them and they come to life as a mighty army. Third, the Lord brings them back into their homeland. Restoration and transformation are complete!

God takes the initiative for our overcoming. Our part is to *proclaim* His Word, *take hold* of His promise, and *experience* its fulfillment. The active working of God's initiative in our lives depends on our ongoing response to His action. Many Christians think victory is a one-time decision made when they first accept the Lord. Being born again is akin to being inducted into the army. It is the key to becoming a conqueror because it personally connects us to the One who has already overcome. In our rebirth the risen Son of God comes to indwell us. How we respond to this induction as well as to the Lord's indwelling will determine whether we experience victory or defeat in our lives. Our new birth in Christ is only the beginning of spiritual life, just as natural birth is the beginning of human life. Growth must follow. I have yet to see a star athlete, a great scholar, a five star general, or a powerful man or woman of God come out of a hospital delivery room!

God's Will and Our Will

Entwined in the will of God as revealed in chapters 36 and 37 of Ezekiel is also His revelation for *our will*. God tells us what our response to His initiative should be. Unfortunately, many believers often treat the work of the Holy Spirit in their lives as if He is the water cooler standing in the corner of the room. Whenever they feel like it, they run over and push a button for a drink. God's presence in our lives is more akin to the old-time water pump that must be primed to get started and used regularly or else it will rust up. Without daily use, the "pipe" leading upward to our thirst from the wellspring of the Holy Spirit deep in the underground of our heart will become empty and dry. Then, when we suddenly need His anointing, the water will not flow. For God's "I wills" to actively and continually manifest in our experience, we must respond to Him daily. Speaking in tongues is one of the best and most useful ways for us to respond. Nothing clears and opens the spiritual "pipeline" better. As we commune in the Spirit we will come into a better knowledge of what God wills for *our* will, as well as a deeper understanding of *how* to exercise our will in the way He desires.

Chapters 36 and 37 of Ezekiel reveal eight "you wills" that God has said we are to aggressively walk out in response to His will:

1. "You shall (will) be clean..."—Ezekiel 36:25b.

2. "You shall (will) dwell in the land that I gave to your fathers"—Ezekiel 36:28a.

3. "You shall (will) be My people..."—Ezekiel 36:28b.

4. "You will remember your evil ways and your deeds that were not good; and you will loathe yourselves in your own sight, for your iniquities and your abominations"—Ezekiel 36:31.

5. "You shall (will) live (physically)"—Ezekiel 37:6b.

6. "You shall (will) know that I am the Lord"—Ezekiel 37:6c.

7. "You shall (will) live (spiritually)"—Ezekiel 37:14b.

8. "You shall (will) know that I, the Lord, have spoken it and performed it"—Ezekiel 37:14d.

How could any reasonable person have a problem lining up his or her will with the will of God as revealed in these passages? God's will is always for our good. That is why the revelation of redemption in Christ is called the *good news*.

In Ezekiel's vision, the Holy Spirit transforms the impossible into the invincible: A valley of dead bones becomes a mighty army. This transformation takes place as obedient faith is combined with the Word of God and the presence of the Holy Spirit. The bones in our physical bodies are held together by muscles and tendons, and all must be cared for regularly in order to function properly. By the same token, we need to bring together the "bones" of our spiritual life in our daily walk by exercising faith, familiarizing ourselves with the Word of God, and communing with Him by praying in the Spirit. When we do these things consistently, the Holy Spirit will bring us victory. We will see God transforming the valley of dry bones in our lives into a mighty army full of the Breath of the Almighty!

Here are some important "bones" that will strengthen our daily spiritual walk:

- *Acknowledge* God's presence and power.

- *Absorb* and digest the Word of God.

- *Speak* the Word of God over our situation.

- *Get* a living word from Scripture for our situation.

- *Write down* every Scripture promise pertaining to our situation.

- *Personalize* the promise of the verse, inserting our name or the names of those for whom we are praying.

- *Serve* the Lord faithfully and patiently while we **wait** for His Word to come to pass.

- *Decide* to let God's Word be the truth in our situation even more than the circumstances in front of our eyes.

- *Accept* that shaking in our circumstances is for our solidification, not for our destruction. Our foundation is a Person, God Himself.

- *Meditate* on God's promises day and night.

- *Obey* their instructions.

- *Keep* them on our tongues. Our conversation must not deny the promises of God's Word.

- *Change our minds* from the slave mentality to the conqueror mentality.

- *Agree* with the Word of God even if it means changing our mind, attitude, and actions about things and people around us.

- *Picture* the Word being accomplished in our lives.

- *Welcome the Holy Spirit* as our daily Guide and Teacher. Pray in tongues daily to keep this link strong.

- *Live* by faith: Start out in faith and keep the vision before us.

- *Expect* a miracle.

- *Refuse* to let go until blessing comes: winners never quit, quitters never win. Don't give up!

Each of these "bones" is an *action* verb. As we put them into action in our daily lives we will find a transformation taking place in those areas where we have longed to experience victory.

Hearing and Overcoming

Hearing and overcoming are intrinsically connected. In Revelation chapters 2 and 3, John records messages from Jesus to seven churches in Asia Minor. Each message concludes with the words, "He who has an ear, let him hear what the Spirit says to the churches," followed by a promise "to him who overcomes." Jesus says essentially the same thing in Mark 4:24: "Take heed what you hear. With the same measure you use, it will be measured to you; and to you who hear, more will be given."

For those who hear His voice, the Lord's promise is very specific: "more will be given." He makes it clear in the very next verse that those who do not heed what they hear will lose whatever they already have. If we are willing to open our ears and hear the voice of the Lord, He will take even what we have, no matter how little or much, and multiply it thirty-, fifty-, or a hundred-fold depending on our faith and obedience. The key to hearing the voice of God (and thereby overcoming and being transformed) is to be hungry and thirsty for His Word and His righteousness. Praying in the Spirit (in tongues) helps sensitize our hearts and minds to hear the Lord's voice and understand His Word.

Hearing and knowing the voice of God lead us into a better understanding of who He really is. He is the Lord, our Savior and Redeemer. He is our Healer. He is our Righteousness and our Peace, our banner of victory. He is the Shepherd of our souls and our Provider. He is One who sets us apart for His purposes. God is all of these and more, all at once. We come to know Him better as the Spirit more and more distills all of these parts of God's character into our understanding. This understanding will affect how we live, how we talk, how we pray, and how we proclaim the good news of Jesus.

God is growing a tree of righteousness in each one of us. He is growing eternal life. He is maturing and transforming those who will reign and rule with Him because they have learned to know His voice over a period of time. They have conformed to His image under His hand and then, when that day comes, they are ready, fit, to sit down beside Him. We need to lay hold of patience and persevere. Luke 21:19 says, "By your patience possess your souls." The Holy Spirit wants to bring the pure Word of God to life in us through the distillation process, and that takes time. We must be willing to undergo His restoration and transformation process; to have His divine breath infuse these old "dry bones" of ours with new life. We who have ears to hear will overcome and sit with Him to reign and rule in His Kingdom.

Chapter Eleven

EQUIPPED FOR BATTLE

It has been said that nature abhors a vacuum. The same is true in the realm of the spirit. Any environment or circumstance of mankind will be governed either by the Spirit of God or the spirit of darkness; there is no middle ground. At least over the short term, which spirit prevails depends largely on the choices that people make.

In the early years of the twentieth century, the pouring out of the Holy through the prayers and preaching of a simple black man named "Papa" Seymour on Azusa Street in Los Angeles, California, resulted in a spiritual phenomenon on a scale unseen since the first century. The birth of the modern Pentecostal movement brought together people of all races, rich and poor, to worship and serve God. Unusual signs and manifestations, including speaking in tongues, accompanied that outpouring. The revival that began at Azusa Street spread across the United States and even crossed the Atlantic Ocean to fall in Wales and other locations in Europe. God was sending a fresh spiritual rain over the earth.

As this spiritual rain front moved across Europe, it arrived in Germany at just the right moment to protect her culture, churches, and people from the spirit of antichrist that was arising in the nation. A Pentecostal revival broke out in the German city of Kassel, but died quickly because of the opposition of German evangelical church leaders. Theologians weighed in, calling on their educational background and human reason in an effort to dissect the work of the third Person of the Godhead. They critically analyzed the phenomenon of the Holy Spirit and the unusual manifestations of these revivals and found them wanting.

In 1909, 56 conservative evangelical German church leaders issued a joint statement called the Berlin Declaration, in which they soundly condemned the Pentecostal movement. The declaration stated, in part:

> This so-called Pentecostal movement is not from above, but from below; many of its phenomena can also be found in spiritism. Demons are at work here who, led by Satan's cunning, mix truth and lies in order to entice the children of God....the personal faith and dedication of some leading brothers and sisters cannot deceive us, not even the healings, tongues, prophecies, etc.....the movement brings forth powerful spiritual and physical manifestations...like falling, face twitching, trembling and shaking, screaming, ugly and loud laughing....such phenomena are not worked by God....The persons transmitting [prophecies] are often women. This had the effect that in some areas women, even young women, stand as leaders in the center of ministry—which is clearly against the Word.

With these and many more references *the German Church refused her only weapon against the spirit of antichrist—the weapon of the anointing.* Five years later, Germany plunged herself and much of the rest of the world into the fiery cauldron of World War I, a conflict that consumed the cream of an entire generation of European manhood. The spiritual vacuum created by Germany's rejection of the Holy Spirit intensified in the economic and social devastation that followed the war, creating an opportunity for the spirit of antichrist to fill the gap with the rise to power of Adolf Hitler and the Nazi party. That evil spirit engulfed the globe in the horror and unbelievable brutality of the Second World War. As a result, 55 million people around the world died.

The spirit realm abhors a vacuum. When individuals, churches, or cultures reject the Holy Spirit, they create a vacuum which the spirit of antichrist rushes to fill.

An Enemy Has Done This

For generations the mere mention of "antichrist" has caused many Christians to faint with fright and look around in confusion. That, however, is the response of a carnal disposition. Ultimately, Christians have no reason to fear the spirit of antichrist or anyone it inhabits. The emergence of persons operating under the influence of the spirit of antichrist is certainly no cause for rejoicing, but we must also recognize that the emergence of this spirit is a sign that Christ is soon to appear. Scripture tells us that as the endtimes unfold, the spirit of antichrist will appear more and more in people, institutions, and government. As the apostle John writes,

> *Little children, it is the last hour; and as you have heard that the Antichrist is coming, even now many antichrists have come, by which we know that it is the last hour. They went out from us, but they were not of us; for if they had been of us, they would have continued with us; but they went out that they might*

be made manifest, that none of them were of us
(1 John 2:18-19).

Not only does John link the increase in the spirit of antichrist with the endtimes, or "the last hour," he also reveals that much of that spirit will arise from within the formal ranks of the church! It had already happened in John's day. For 2,000 years, every generation of the Church has had false believers, wolves disguised as sheep, mingling among the flock of the Lord's faithful. It is still true today and will continue to be so. There will be tares among the wheat until Jesus returns.

John describes an antichrist as anyone who "denies the Father and the Son" (1 Jn. 2:22). The spirit of antichrist stands in absolute opposition to God and His ways: "Every spirit that does not confess that Jesus Christ has come in the flesh is not of God. And this is the spirit of the antichrist, which you have heard was coming, and is now already in the world" (1 Jn. 4:3); "For many deceivers have gone out into the world who do not confess Jesus Christ as coming in the flesh. This is a deceiver and an antichrist" (2 Jn. 1:7).

Today there is a fresh emergence of the spirit of antichrist around the world. In recent years new expressions of anti-Christian and anti-Semitic hatred have appeared. Innocent Jews and Christians have been and continue to be murdered in some nations. Synagogues are desecrated, churches are destroyed, and acts of religious terror multiply across the globe. Anti-Semitism is a sign of the spirit of antichrist. It is impossible to love and support the Son of God while at the same time hating the chosen people of God, the people through whose human lineage the Son of God came to earth.

Certainly one of the most potent demonstrations of the spirit of antichrist in our day took place on September 11, 2001. The hatred and murderous violence spawned by Osama bin Laden and the members of the al-Qaeda terrorist network is inspired by a spiritual enemy who hates God and everything God stands for. Anyone or anything that denies Christ serves the spirit of antichrist. Violent, radical, militant Islamic fundamentalism meets this description. This helps explain the implacable hostility that many radical Islamicists have toward the nation of Israel. Because the spirit of antichrist hates God, it also hates His Son and His people. The nation of Israel lives under the menace of that hatred every day.

Terrorists such as those in al-Qaeda endanger not only Americans, but people of every nation. Their hatred acknowledges no geographical boundaries. They truly are a global threat.

When the terrorist attacks came on 9-11, I sensed the Lord saying very clearly to me, "An enemy has done this." This is the same thing the man In Jesus' parable said to his servants when he discovered that tares had been secretly sown with his wheat (see Mt. 13:24-30). Soon after the attacks, some prominent Christian leaders pronounced that they were a sign of God's judgment on America. As much as I love and respect those men as Christian brothers, I could not disagree with them more on this point. What happened on 9-11 was nothing other than the murderous hatred of the spirit of antichrist expressing itself. The enemy is very jealous and fearful of America's potential under the call of God as a beacon of freedom to the world, as a great reservoir from which the gospel is sent out across the earth and, especially, as a friend to Israel.

Our nation is a "first strike" target for satan, the adversary. Derailing the cause of Christ and destroying the nation of Israel are also at the top of his list. An enemy is at work against God, His people, and His ways. Now is not the time to get caught up in declaring judgment on ourselves or each other. Now is the time for us to connect with the power of God.

Anointing—the Secret Weapon of the Church

J esus promised that when the Holy Spirit came we would receive power. It is very important for us to connect in our hearts and minds the endtimes Church with the power of God, because the battle of the last days will be between the power of the Holy Spirit and the power of the spirit of antichrist.

How can we as Christians discern and be preserved from the spirit of antichrist? What is our secret for power and victory as the Kingdom of God and the kingdom of satan oppose one another? The answer lies in Jesus' promise, "You shall receive power when the Holy Spirit has come upon you" (Acts 1:8a). First John 2:20 says that we have "an anointing from the Holy One." This anointing seals and preserves us, and helps us "know all things." Through the anointing the Spirit of God will equip us with everything we need to face the spirit of antichrist.

While we should always honor, respect, and appreciate valid sacred tradition and correct doctrine, these alone will not protect us from the spirit of antichrist. In fact, as we see from history, they can create a false sense of security that leaves room for deception and destruction. Ultimately, our understanding of the Kingdom of God and our protection against the spirit of antichrist will not come from accurate theology or sound teaching *alone*. We need *power*. We need *discernment*. Our seal, our protection, our knowledge, our discernment, and our power come from the anointing of the Holy Spirit.

The anointing of the Holy Spirit is the secret weapon of the church. As we look toward the end of the age it is absolutely imperative that we welcome the move of the Holy

Spirit and learn to steward His Presence. Through the anointing, He will cover us, preserve us, and prepare us to be the Bride of Jesus Christ. The anointing will make manifest the glory of the Lord. The anointing will take us triumphantly home!

Under our "anointing from the Holy One" we will come to know "all things" pertaining to our battle with the spirit of antichrist. When we bring it to bear, the anointing breaks the yokes of hatred, racism, bigotry, anti-Semitism, and every other stronghold of the powers of darkness. The Lord has issued a call to all people, "Come, stand by My side in the last day." Battle lines have been drawn, and each person must decide whether he or she will stand for Christ or for antichrist. There is no middle road. Jesus said, "He who is not with Me is against Me, and he who does not gather with Me scatters abroad" (Mt. 12:30).

Whether we like it or not, we cannot be neutral with regard to the anointing. Neutrality creates a vacuum of indifference that will quickly be filled by the spirit of darkness. Each of us must make a decision one way or another.

According to legend, in the early days of the battle of the Alamo in San Antonio, Texas in 1836, Colonel William Travis, commander of the fort, drew a line in the sand with his sword and challenged his men to decide whether they would stay and fight or leave. Those who wanted to stay were to step across the line. Inside the fort was a garrison of 180 men; outside were 5,000 Mexican soldiers. To a man, every defender crossed the line. They committed themselves to their cause, even to the point of death.

That's the way it is with us and the anointing. Each of us must eventually commit ourselves to being either for or against the anointing. We cannot straddle the fence, saying, "I accept *this* manifestation of the Spirit, but not *that* one. We cannot say, "Prophecy is all right, but tongues? That's going too far!" The anointing of the Holy Spirit is a "package deal."

Speaking in Tongues Establishes a Holy Atmosphere

We need the Spirit's anointing to help us connect to the power of God for victory over the spirit of antichrist that we encounter in the business of everyday life. One of the best ways to activate the anointing is by praying in the Spirit. Speaking in tongues is like a spiritual "gas mask" that filters out the noxious fumes that satan spews out to poison our spirits, our homes, and our families.

One of satan's most potent poisons is fear. On September 11, 2001, Americans experienced fear at a whole new level. The ongoing threat of terrorist attacks in this country has given us a taste of the kind of anxiety people in many other countries live with on a daily basis. Fear can paralyze, demoralize, and even kill. Fear can cause someone to keep silent when he should speak up. Fear spawns hatred, bigotry, hostility, and conflict.

We need to breathe the clean, pure air of the Holy Spirit, and praying in tongues is a cleanser that helps purge the spiritual "grunge" that has built up in our hearts. Praying in the Spirit is like walking on the beach at sunrise or climbing to the top of a mountain and taking in great draughts of the clear alpine air. As we pray, the sickening, toxic fumes from the devil begin to dissipate. Speaking in tongues is a way to allow the Holy Spirit to saturate and fill every pore of our being, body, soul, and spirit. It helps establish a holy atmosphere around us and those for whom we pray.

We have a responsibility to monitor and, if necessary, change the atmosphere in our homes. Fear, anxiety, depression, and other noxious gases from the devil invade our homes through television, radio, the internet, books, magazines, and newspapers. Bad news and frightful situations assault our senses on a daily basis. Prayer can change the atmosphere—prayer that exalts the name of Jesus. In the power of the Spirit, we can declare, "I don't care who the terrorist is—Hitler, Stalin, or Osama bin Laden; I don't care where the fear came from; Jesus Christ is the same yesterday, today, and forever. He is the Lion of the tribe of Judah, King of kings and Lord of lords, and He is in charge."

It's okay to listen to the news, as long as we allow the anointing of the Spirit to help us keep a holy and godly perspective. As we develop the practice of speaking in tongues regularly and rebuking the evil manifestations of the spirit of antichrist, we will change the spiritual atmosphere around us.

Speaking in tongues calls forth the resources and power of the Spirit of God to confound the forces of darkness. There is a thrilling sequence in the film *The Lord of the Rings: The Fellowship of the Ring* that illustrates this truth.

Frodo, the young hobbit who is carrying the One Ring of power has been grievously wounded by the Nazgul, phantom-like horsemen and servants of the dark lord, Sauron. Frodo's companions are concerned that he will die before they can get him to safety. Suddenly, a beautiful elf princess named Arwen appears within a brilliance of light and begins to encourage Frodo in this unknown tongue saying, "I am Arwen, I've come to help you. Hear my voice, come back to the light."

Taking Frodo in her arms, Arwen again speaks in this unknown language, commanding her white horse, "Noro lim, noro lim, Asfaloth!" She then dashes off on her swift horse with the Nazgul in hot pursuit. Crossing the river into Rivendell, the elf domain where she lives and where safety for Frodo lies, Arwen draws her sword, and turns to face the Nazgul as they hesitate on the far side of the river. Boldly, she issues a challenge: "If you want him, come and claim him!"

As the Nazgul urge their horses into the river, Arwen calls out once more in the unknown tongue, which is her own elfish language. In the midst of the river the Princess begins to speak into it this heavenly language. The power of the river is released, and Arwen's very being is empowered by the strength of its waters. The river rises rapidly to a flood, and white-crested waves in the shape of beautiful white horses sweep the Nazgul and their mounts away in the rushing torrent. Frodo is safe, and Arwen is able to impart a measure of healing to him.

My spirit bore witness to the prophetic depiction this scene inspired. For me it was a picture of the Lord's Bride in the last days; holding up the sword of the Spirit and praying in an unknown tongue. I see this as a prophetic picture of the last-day Church, and the potential of the nations being rescued and brought into the light of the gospel of the Lord Jesus Christ. We are to take the "little ones," Israel and all the lost peoples of the nations, in our "arms" of prayer. As the Bride of Christ we are to protect the modern nation of Israel with our prayers, and speak in that heavenly language, releasing the power of the river of God to sweep away the enemy. Psalm 122:6 charges us to "Pray for the peace of Jerusalem." We are to be ever watchful in prayer. May the Bride of Christ hold in her arms not only Israel, but all the hurting, oppressed peoples needing salvation and deliverance.

Ezekiel chapter 47 pictures a great river flowing out from the temple of the Lord which quickly becomes too deep and wide to cross, and everything touched by the river becomes vibrant with life. Jesus spoke of the Holy Spirit as "rivers of living water" that would flow out of our hearts.

The only one who can fully release the Holy Spirit is the divine royal princess called the Bride of Christ. *We* are the Bride of Christ—everyone who believes on Him. United under the common anointing of the Holy Spirit, and with our Bridegroom at our head, we become a force that all the powers of darkness cannot withstand. There is strength in numbers. The devil has tried to attack us in different ways because he is scared to death of "Holy Ghost" people. We know how to plug into the power of God. We believe in the baptism of the Holy Spirit. We believe in healing. We believe in deliverance. We believe in the laying on of hands. We believe in victory, because Jesus Christ is the same yesterday, today, and forever.

We are strongest when we come together as one body, because then we can use the greatest weapon in our spiritual arsenal: *corporate prayer*.

The Power of Corporate Prayer

We are living, I believe, in the most critical generation in human history. Never before have the opportunities and challenges for God's people been so great or the stakes so high. The Lord is calling us to take our places as watchmen on the wall, as in the Book of Isaiah:

> *I have set watchmen on your walls, O Jerusalem;*
> *they shall never hold their peace day or night. You*
> *who make mention of the Lord, do not keep silent,*
> *and give Him no rest till He establishes and till He*
> *makes Jerusalem a praise in the earth* (Isaiah 62:6-7).

There is a crying need for us to "stand in the gap" (see Ezek. 22:30) as intercessors for each other, for the unsaved, for our families, and for our country, and to do battle against the satanic powers in the heavenlies that are set to inflict harm on America, on Israel, and on all the nations.

In terms of our lives as disciples of Christ, prayer is where everything begins and ends. Nothing God wills to do on earth will happen without prayer. On the other hand, when believers pray, particularly in concert with one another, nothing is impossible. Jesus said, "...if two of you agree on earth concerning anything that they ask, it will be done for them by My Father in heaven. For where two or three are gathered together in My name, I am there in the midst of them" (Mt. 18:19-20).

What an awesome promise this is! Do we truly comprehend the magnitude of what is available to us? Other than the Lord Himself, no power or principality in either the natural or spiritual realms can match the power of His people united in corporate prayer. What's more, anybody can pray! There are no special qualifications or age restrictions. God hears every prayer of faith, whether from the lips of an old saint who has walked long and far with Him, or the youngest child who is just beginning the journey.

Yes, anyone can pray, but in truth, hardly anyone really wants to. Consistent, persistent prayer is difficult, particularly intercession. It requires commitment, time, sacrifice, and discipline. In a shallow, superficial, and 30-second-sound-bite-accustomed culture such as ours, these are costly concepts, even for many believers.

Nevertheless, God is calling us to the corporate experience of prayer. In Matthew 18:19, Jesus promised that whoever could "agree" together concerning what they asked for would receive it from the Father. The word "agree" also means "harmonize." If we "harmonize" together in prayer, God will do it. We cannot harmonize, however, unless we first come together in the place of prayer and reach a oneness of mind, spirit, and purpose. This does not mean we have to be in lock-step and see eye-to-eye on every little thing, but that we are united in the common love, grace, and anointing of the Spirit. The Holy Spirit can bring harmony in the midst of diversity, and bring us all into oneness with the heart and mind of the Father.

Christ's call to His Church today is for corporate prayer—intimate communion with Him and intercession that moves heaven and earth for the purposes of God. Through corporate prayer, as with private prayer, we come to know the Lord, so that when we stand before Him on that day, having cast out demons, healed the sick, preached the gospel, and done all manner of other wonderful works in His name, He will know us because we have been with Him regularly in the place of prayer. Then He will say, "Well done, good and faithful servant; you were faithful over a few things, I will make you ruler over many things. Enter into the joy of your lord" (Mt. 25:21).

The Holy Spirit is so efficient. He is the God of miracles, not tied down by limitations of time and space. He has given us some amazing tools. One of the best of these is speaking in tongues, which allows the altar of prayer to be open always in our lives, enabling us also to enter into the higher realm of Spirit-anointed corporate prayer.

Acts 12:1-17 provides one of the best examples in Scripture of the power of corporate prayer. Herod Antipas had arrested the apostle Peter and put him in prison, planning to bring him out before the Jews after Passover and execute him, as he had already done to James, John's brother. Verse 5 states simply, "Peter was therefore kept in prison, but constant prayer was offered to God for him by the church." As a result, an angel appeared to release Peter. Peter's chains fell off of their own accord. The angel led Peter past the sleeping guards to the outer iron gate, which opened by itself. Outside was the street and freedom, and there the angel departed.

Peter's deliverance was directly related to the corporate prayer of the Church. A similar demonstration of the power of corporate prayer is found in chapter 4 of Acts when the Church, in response to increasing opposition and persecution, prays to the Lord for boldness in witness and preaching and for signs and wonders to be done in His name. The result of their prayer is recorded in verse 31: "And when they had prayed, the place where they were assembled together was shaken; and they were all filled with the Holy Spirit, and they spoke the word of God with boldness."

Corporate prayer is our greatest weapon against the spirit of antichrist. The powers of darkness cannot stand against the assault of God's people praying with one accord in the power and anointing of the Spirit. That is why satan desperately works to distract, divide, and destroy the unity of the Body of Christ *before* we come to the place of prayer. Unfortunately, he is successful much of the time.

Watchmen, To the Walls!

Just as the Great Wall of China is visible to the naked eye from earth orbit, I believe that when God gazes down from Heaven, the one thing He looks for is a great wall of prayer from His people, surrounding the nations of the earth. He wants to see a mighty battlement of intercession protecting the unsaved millions in the world from the deception and bondage of satan.

Any defensive wall must be manned and kept in good repair if it is to be effective in keeping out the enemy. Sadly, the church's wall of intercession is in serious disrepair. It has been generations since all the watchmen were on the wall in their places. All it takes is one or two inattentive watchmen to give an advantage to the enemy. During those generations, satan and his legions have breached the wall in numerous places and carried off many souls who are helpless without the light of Christ.

It is time for us to man our posts, repair the breaches, and close the wall of intercession surrounding the nations. Our corporate prayers in the Spirit are the bricks, and the anointing of God is the mortar. Such a wall is unassailable. It is also indispensable. Whenever the hand of God moves for the nations, it is in response to corporate prayer. No great revival, spiritual awakening, or divine visitation ever occurred—from Abraham to Moses to Jesus to Pentecost to Azusa Street to Wales and beyond—that was not first precipitated by intercessors gathering together in corporate prayer, tarrying before the living God, refusing to let the battle flag fall to the ground, no matter what the opposition.

God has called us—you and me—to intercede for the nations. We say we want to be where God is. Well, God is where prayer is, and He is especially present in the environment of corporate prayer. A body of committed believers praying in harmony together in the Spirit connect with the glory of God and create an atmosphere in which He is pleased to dwell.

Nothing benefits the Body of Christ more or disciples us in the practical matters of Christian living more quickly than to be involved regularly in corporate fellowship, prayer, and intercession. The writer of Hebrews encourages us to "consider one another in order to stir up love and good works, not forsaking the assembling of ourselves together, as is the manner of some, but exhorting one another, and so much the more as you see the Day approaching" (Heb. 10:24-25). Now is not the time for inattention and slumber. As watchmen praying for our children, our grandchildren, and concerns regarding our nation, we are needed on the wall, alert and ready.

When we get to the place where we can sit and wait on God for hours at a time in the context of the believing community, with brothers and sisters praying, sharing their revelations and burden, and joining together in one mind and spirit, things in us will start to change. Our perspective, our understanding, our endurance, our patience, our perseverance, our hearts, our compassion, our priorities—all of these will go through a metamorphosis, like a caterpillar changing into a butterfly. Corporate prayer is God's practical discipling tool. The Lord is very economical in everything that He does and this is a discipleship program in the truest and deepest sense of the word.

Corporate prayer lies at the heart of what the Lord desires for His people because it brings us into unity and sets us into our proper places as watchmen for the saving of the nations. In this, it is one of God's great mysteries. For generations, we have tried everything in the Church to promote unity and have ended up more divided than ever. Corporate prayer under the anointing of the Spirit brings believers of all stripes together under one banner in a way that nothing else does. As this movement spreads and takes root, it will cross denominational lines and transcend charismatic and non-charismatic persuasions.

It has already begun to do so. At All Nations Church, where Bonnie and I are pastors, we have been engaged for several years now in a weekly gathering called The Watch of the Lord. Every Friday night our congregation comes together for an all-night vigil of prayer and intercession for our nation, the nation of Israel, and for all the peoples of the world. We are trying to be faithful to our responsibility as watchmen on the wall. Since we began this prayer ministry, other churches have partnered with us until today, worldwide, hundreds of congregations are linked to us directly in The Watch of the Lord prayer movement. At this writing, approximately two million hours of prayer monthly are going up through this movement globally.

Watch and Pray

We are the Church of the new millennium—all of us who are committed to the Lord Jesus Christ. We are the end-times generation, the Bride of Christ looking with great anticipation for the coming of our Bridegroom. Ours must not be an idle waiting, however. Our Lord has given us a great commission to proclaim the gospel and make disciples of all nations. He has charged us with the "ministry of reconciliation" (2 Cor. 5:18b) by which we become His instruments for reconciling a lost world to God. The challenges are great, the stakes are high, and we have a crafty and dangerous enemy who "walks about like a roaring lion, seeking whom he may devour" (1 Pet. 5:8b).

For these reasons, we need to be men and women of discernment. We must learn to flow in the anointing of the Lord, seeing in the Spirit, hearing in the Spirit, and praying in the Spirit. The Word of God is our foundation, guiding us so that we do not walk in confusion or error. The Holy Spirit illuminates our soul to understand the Word of God so that we do not walk in darkness. His anointing brings us into harmony with the heart and mind of God. He gives us a prayer language that enables us to commune with our Father at a level deeper than human consciousness.

The hidden power of speaking in tongues is that it allows us to touch the very heart and mind of God to move heaven and earth in response to our prayers. It enables us to sing the melody of Heaven and bring a taste of divine glory into our everyday experience. Speaking in tongues reveals its greatest potency in the collective atmosphere of corporate prayer. No power on earth is stronger than Christian believers praying in the Spirit in one accord with one mind and one heart. This is the secret to confronting the spirit of antichrist.

Jesus is coming again. His return is certain, although no one but the Father knows the day or the hour. As that day approaches, the work of the spirit of antichrist will intensify, and the alertness and steadfastness of the watchmen of the Lord must intensify as well. We are in a time of war! We cannot afford to be indifferent, inattentive, or uninvolved. As followers of Christ, we are soldiers in His army, and His Spirit has equipped us with everything we need for battle. Prayer and the Word of God are our most potent weapons. Against them none of the forces of the enemy can stand.

We must be ever vigilant and actively engaged. Our enemy will never rest, and neither should we. "He who is in [us] is greater than he who is in the world" (1 Jn. 4:4b) and the victory is already ours through Christ our Lord. Jesus said of His coming, "But of that day and hour no one knows, not even the angels in heaven, nor the Son, but only the Father. Take heed, watch and pray; for you do not know when the time is" (Mk. 13:32-33).

We do not know the day or the hour, but we do know what we are to do in the meantime: Preach the gospel, make disciples, and *watch and pray*!

⁕

A Prayer to receive the infilling of the Holy Spirit with speaking in tongues.

The first step in receiving the Holy Spirit is to repent and receive Christ Jesus as your Lord and Savior. According to the Bible, we are all sinners:

For all have sinned and fall short of the glory of God (Romans 3:23).

This applies to all people in every nation.

The penalty for sin is death:

For the wages of sin is death, but the gift of God is eternal life in Christ Jesus our Lord (Romans 6:23).

God graciously gave His Son Jesus Christ to take the punishment for our sins:

But God demonstrates His own love toward us, in that while we were still sinners, Christ died for us (Romans 5:8).

In Him we have redemption through His blood, the forgiveness of sins, according to the riches of His grace (Ephesians 1:7).

Jesus died for our sins, but rose from the dead three days later:

I am He who lives, and was dead, and behold, I am alive forevermore. Amen. And I have the keys of Hades and of Death (Revelation 1:18).

You may receive salvation and experience a new spiritual birth through faith in Jesus Christ:

If you confess with your mouth the Lord Jesus and believe in your heart that God has raised Him from the dead, you will be saved (Romans 10:9).

For by grace you have been saved through faith, and that not of yourselves; it is the gift of God, not of works lest anyone should boast (Ephesians 2:8-9).

He who believes in the Son has everlasting life; and he who does not believe the Son shall not see life, but the wrath of God abides on him (John 3:36).

To Him all the prophets witness that, through His name, however believes in Him will receive remission of sins (Acts 10:43).

Come to the Lord Jesus in repentance for all your sins. He will not turn you away:

And the Spirit and the bride say, "Come!" And let him who hears say, "Come!" And let him who thirsts come. Whoever desires, let him take the water of life freely (Revelation 22:17).

I pray that you will truly have the grace to turn your back on all sin, which is the meaning of repentance. As you affirm the above truths, then by faith accept the promise of the Holy Spirit according to Scripture:

Then Peter said to them, "Repent, and let every one of you be baptized in the name of Jesus Christ for the remission of sins; and you shall receive the gift of the Holy Spirit" (Acts 2:38).

Pray the following prayer and mean it with all your heart:

Dear heavenly Father, I thank you for sending Your Son Jesus Christ to die on the cross for my sins. I believe He died, was buried, and on the third day rose again from the dead. I do repent of my sins and come to You for mercy and forgiveness. I renounce satan and the kingdom of darkness. I break every family curse over my family and me. By faith in Your promise, I receive Jesus Christ personally as my Savior and confess Him as my Lord. Come in to my heart, Lord Jesus, and give me eternal life and make me a child of God. Thank You Lord for accepting me and now, Lord Jesus, I am thirsty for more of You. I ask You, Lord Jesus, to baptize me in Your Holy Spirit with the evidence of speaking in tongues. By faith I receive Your Holy Spirit now. In the name of Jesus Christ I pray. Amen.

As you pray this prayer, take a deep breath. In fact, take several deep breaths. God keeps His Word, and He will fill you with His wonderful Holy Spirit. Acts 2:4 says, "And they were all filled with the Holy Spirit and began to speak with other tongues, as the Spirit gave them utterance." I encourage you to open your mouth and speak. As your voice proceeds, the Holy Spirit will begin to give you words. They may be words you have never heard before. Do not be concerned with what you are saying, because you are speaking not by intellect but through your spirit.

In my experience it is easier to do than to explain. Remember, receiving the Holy Spirit and speaking in tongues is an act of faith. You are appropriating a mighty promise of God. You may not feel anything. Some have emotional experiences, but this is not necessary. Just begin to speak, even if you only have a few words. Persevere. After a time, there will be a strong flow. Some get immediate fluency while others get only a few words initially. Either way, it is coming from the Spirit of God, so thank Him. Be persistent! On occasion, people get self-conscious and do not get a full release until sometime later, but I encourage you to persist. Believe me it is worth the effort! Begin to praise and thank the Lord.

For other books, audiotapes, or other resource material from the author, contact:

Mahesh Chavda Ministries International
P.O. Box 411008
Charlotte, NC 28241
(704) 543-7272
FAX: (704) 541-5300

E-mail: info@watchofthelord.com
www.watchofthelord.com

Books by Mahesh Chavda

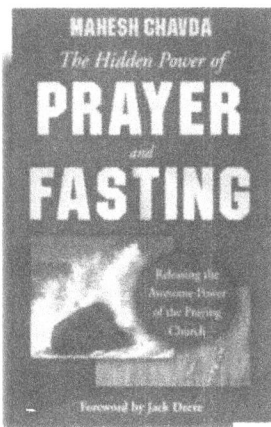

THE HIDDEN POWER OF PRAYER AND FASTING

The praying believer is the confident believer. But the fasting believer is the overcoming believer. This is the believer who changes the circumstances and the world around him. He is the one who experiences the supernatural power of the risen Lord in his everyday life. An international evangelist and the senior pastor of All Nations Church in Charlotte, North Carolina, Mahesh Chavda has seen firsthand the power of God released through a lifestyle of prayer and fasting. Here he shares from decades of personal experience and scriptural study principles and practical tips about fasting and praying. This book will inspire you to tap into God's power and change your life, your city, and your nation!

ISBN: 0-7684-2017-2

THE HIDDEN POWER OF THE BELIEVER'S TOUCH

Here is the fatal blow to the belief that God does not heal today. Through the power of his personal experience and the strength of his biblical insight. Mahesh Chavda reveals how the healing compassion of our Lord reaches the hurting masses simply by the believer's healing touch. Written with compassion, humor, and insight, *The Hidden Power of the Believer's Touch* affirms that the healing anointing and the gifts of signs and wonders are not reserved for "super saints" or the specially gifted, but are available to every believer who carries the compassion and love of the Lord Jesus.

ISBN: 0-7684-1974-3

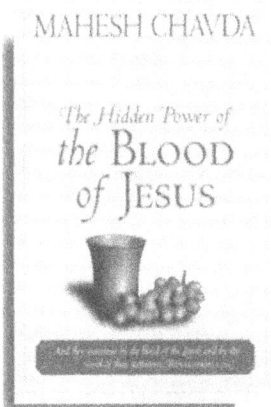

THE HIDDEN POWER OF THE BLOOD OF JESUS

In this pop Christian culture many believers have never been exposed to the great truths upon which the Church of Jesus Christ has been built. One of those forgotten truths is the purpose and power of the blood of Jesus. We sing about it in our hymns, there is power in the blood, but few of us have experienced the realty of those words.

Chavda carefully lays the foundation as he presents a refreshing look at the importance of the blood of Jesus in the life of the believer. *The Hidden Power of the Blood of Jesus* is theologically sound but passionately written in a way that the reader will gasp for air as he discovers each new truth. Chavda will transform your thinking on the blood of Jesus as he lifts it out of its stuffy theological setting and makes it practical in your life.

ISBN: 0-7684-2222-1

Available at your local Christian bookstore.

For more information and sample chapters, visit www.destinyimage.com

D Destiny Image

DESTINY IMAGE PUBLISHERS, INC.

*"Speaking to the Purposes of God for This Generation
and for the Generations to Come."*

VISIT OUR NEW SITE HOME AT
WWW.DESTINYIMAGE.COM

FREE SUBSCRIPTION TO DI NEWSLETTER

Receive free unpublished articles by top DI authors, exclusive
discounts, and free downloads from our best and newest books.

Visit www.destinyimage.com to subscribe.

Write to: Destiny Image
P.O. Box 310
Shippensburg, PA 17257-0310

Call: 1-800-722-6774

Email: orders@destinyimage.com

For a complete list of our titles or to place an order
online, visit www.destinyimage.com.

FIND US ON FACEBOOK OR FOLLOW US ON TWITTER.

www.facebook.com/destinyimage   facebook
www.twitter.com/destinyimage   twitter